Contents

Acknowledgments   vii

Introduction: Games and Brains   1

**1   The Use of Games and Activities
        in the World of Meetings   5**

Let's Look at Meetings   8

Time-Tested Tips for Better Meetings   8

Characteristics of Games and Activities   11

Suggestions for the Use of Games   12

Some Caveats   13

Games: Brain Teaser #1   15
           Brainstorming   19
           Creative People I Have Known   21
           Six Thinking Hats (Group Perspective)   23
           Six Thinking Hats (Individual Perspective)   27
           Who's on First?   31

**2   Brain "Very" Basics:
        What Does It Look Like?   37**

Basic Structure of the Brain   40

Left Brain–Right Brain Specialization   43

Games: Disney's Four Cs of Creativity   49
           All in the Family   51
           Wanna Go for a Ride?   55
           Take a Letter   57
           One Word at a Time   59
           Stand Up–Sit Down   61

3   Brain Myths: Separating Fact from Fiction   63

We Use Only 10 Percent of Our Brain   65

Some People Are Left-Brained; Some People Are
   Right-Brained   66

Multitasking Saves Time   67

Drinking Alcohol Kills Brain Cells   68

You Can't Grow New Brain Cells   69

Fact or Fiction?   70

Games: Brain Teaser #2   71
         You Can't Teach an Old Dog . . .   75
         IQ vs. EQ   77
         Right Brain, Left Brain?   79
         What If?   81
         The Dead Moose Society   83

4   May I Have Your Attention! Make the Move from Attention to Memory   87

Models and Theories of Attention   90

Improving and Enhancing Attention   92

Games: Brain Teaser #3   95
         Just Leave Me Alone   99
         The Alphabet Game   101
         The Official Stand-Up Person   103

5   Where Did I Put My Keys? Help Your Brain Capture and Store Information   105

The Memory Process   107

Memory Retrieval   110

The
big book
of **brain**
building
games

*Fun Activities to Stimulate the Brain—for Better Group
Learning, Communication, and Understanding*

Edward E. Scannell & Carol A. Burnett

Mc
Graw
Hill

New York Chicago San Francisco Lisbon London Madrid Mexico City
Milan New Delhi San Juan Seoul Singapore Sydney Toronto

Library of Congress Cataloging-in-Publication Data

Scannell, Edward E.
    The big book of brain-building games : fun activities to stimulate the brain—for better group learning, communication, and understanding / Edward Scannell and Carol Burnett.
        p.   cm.
    Includes bibliographical references.
    ISBN 978-0-07-163522-6
    1. Management games.   2. Small groups.   3. Group relations training.   4. Cognition—Problems, exercises, etc.   5. Intellect—Problems, exercises, etc.   I. Burnett, Carol (Carol A.), 1947–   II. Title.

HD30.26.S33   2009
658.3'124—dc22   2009027009

1 2 3 4 5 6 7 8 9 10 11 12 13 14 15 16 17 18 19 20 21 22   DOC/DOC   0 9

ISBN 978-0-07-163522-6
MHID   0-07-163522-X

Interior design by Think Book Works
Illustrations by Ryan Allen (www.ryanallen.com)

McGraw-Hill books are available at special quantity discounts to use as premiums and sales promotions or for use in corporate training programs. To contact a representative, please e-mail us at bulksales@mcgraw-hill.com.

Tip of the Tongue   111

Use It or Lose It!   112

Tips for Promoting Memory Retention   113

Games: Are You Smarter than a Ten-Year-Old?   117
         I Can Dream, Can't I?   119
         Hi, There—Next! Part 1   121
         Hi, There—Next! Part 2   123
         Thanks for the Memories   125
         When I Was a Kid . . .   131

6   Adult Learning: Help Your Brain Adapt to Changing Situations   133

Effective Meetings   136

Theories of Adult Learning   137

Laws of Adult Learning   140

Generational Learning Styles   143

Ready, Set, Action   145

Games: Sooo, Howyadune? (Verbal Feedback
         Version)   147
         Sooo, Howyadune? (Visual Feedback
         Version)   149
         I Wish, I Wish   153
         The Law of Effect   155
         Actions Speak Louder than Words   157
         Instant Experts   159
         Dealing with Change   161

7   He Said, She Said: Explore Gender Differences in Learning   163

Structural Differences   166

Functional Differences   167

Games: Brain Teaser #4   175
        Male-Female Brains   179
        Male-Female Perceptions   181
        Circle of Inclusion   183
        My, How You've Changed!   185
        Made to Stick   187

**8   Full Brain Fitness: Enhance and
      Enrich Brain Function   191**

Gifts to Give Your Brain   194

Brain Aerobics   203

Games: Mind Mapping   205
        Want to Be a Genius?   207
        Stress-Stress-Stress!   213
        The Psychology of Change   215
        Take a Card, Any Card   217
        Communication Styles   219
        Top of the Morning   225

Bibliography   227

Acknowledgments

Since the first book in the *Games Trainers Play* series was published some twenty-five years ago, overall sales of that book and subsequent series (*More Games* and *The Big Book*) have exceeded a million copies. With this new book, there are now twelve titles in that series. For this, we are indebted to the thousands of friends and colleagues who have attended workshops and seminars with such groups as the American Society for Training and Development (ASTD), Meeting Professionals International (MPI), and National Speakers Association (NSA), as well as other associations and corporate groups. Coupled with our HRD and HRM audiences across the globe, from "Old" Athens to New Zealand, these audiences have helped us field-test the activities and exercises contained in this book.

On a personal note, a huge debt of gratitude goes to my son and daughters—Mike, Mary, Karen, and Cathie—who have given me their support, love, and encouragement and made their dad a very proud father indeed!

—Edward E. Scannell

I wish to express my sincere gratitude to the following people (and their magnificent brains) whose friendship, leadership, and mentoring have contributed directly, indirectly, and often unknowingly to this book: a special thank you to Bob Lewis, Michael Young, Rob Till, Joe Krokrowoiak, Ed Starr, Mary Helen Albrecht, Bonnie Buell, and to my precious friend Nancy Richbart; to all my students and learners from the United States, Canada, and Spain who have in turn assisted me in the learning process; thanks to my wise, compassionate, and loving daughters, Shannon and Beth, who have always challenged my brain, warmed my heart, and served as my cheerleaders; to my loving and supportive siblings, Chuck, Fran, Bev, Chris, and Steve, who appreciate and embrace the concept of "safety in numbers," thank you for your lifelong encouragement; to all the dedicated brain scientists, researchers, and specialists who have and continue to devotingly utilize their brains in an effort to help the rest of us understand and care for ours—thank you, all.

—*Carol A. Burnett*

Note: Carol and I would both like to give special thanks to Mary Scannell, who was helpful in assisting us with layout, proofreading, and overall assistance; Colleen Fellin, who researched the hundreds of references for us and helped compile the bibliography; and Ryan Allen, whose creativity and ingenuity you will see sprinkled throughout these pages. Thanks also go to Dr. Joanne Sujansky whose encouragement kept us going. Finally, a special note of thanks to Emily Carlton, our editor, and Charles Fisher, senior project editor, whose detail to attention made the final manuscript "ready to roll." We thank you for all your assistance!

Introduction
Games and Brains

You can discover more about a person in an hour of play than in a year of discussion.

—Plato

Research has proven time and again that games, activities, and exercises add spark and excitement to training sessions and help participants achieve dramatically better learning results. The real learning, of course, is not in the game itself but in the process of the activity.

Experienced human resource development professionals, trainers, and meeting planners know full well the value of engaging their audiences in active participation and have used this learning methodology in some of the following ways:

- games to develop leadership ability and build self-confidence
- brain teasers that enhance problem-solving skills and boost creativity
- exercises that teach people to be cooperative and enthusiastic team players
- games that dramatically improve communications skills—from speaking in public to knowing how to listen
- icebreakers guaranteed to grab and hold any group's attention

This book offers a component never before included in a volume filled with such games, puzzles, and exercises. Each chapter introduces state-of-the-art (but easy-to-understand) summaries of specific recent biological, physiological, cognitive, and behavioral research on the brain—and how that research relates to the learning process. The activities that follow each of the chapters will demonstrate, reinforce, and validate the ever-changing plasticity of the brain.

So, why combine brains and games? Recently, the media seem to be infatuated with the brain—how the brain functions, how it ages, and how to nurture, nourish, and strengthen the brain.

Until recently, brain research was limited to exploring how diseased, dysfunctional, or injured brains functioned. Researchers didn't have non-invasive, safe techniques to delve into the inner workings of the healthy brain (beneath the skull) until the mid-1980s. But aided by cutting-edge technologies, today's neuroscientists have propelled us forward in our approach to thinking and learning about our brains.

The Brain Fitness Revolution is here. This exciting frontier signifies a new era—*a brain-new world.*

How to Use This Book

Happily, you will find that most training audiences today not only enjoy taking part in these experiential activities but also expect them to be an integral part of their lifelong learning process.

These types of exercises have multiple uses. First and foremost, they are an absolute necessity as climate setters. The importance of first impressions is well documented, and it is imperative that some kind of get-acquainted exercise be used early in any workshop, or even during the keynote presentation. This will set the tone for the rest of the event. So make certain that those first few minutes include some kind of welcoming activity. This could be as simple as a "meet and greet," a brief way of meeting new friends, or a longer networking game. In any event, allow ample time for this warm-up at the beginning of your sessions.

If it's a workshop you're running, you'll want to incorporate additional games throughout your program. These can take the form of motivating and team-building exercises, which create a fertile atmosphere for handling change, creativity, and problem-solving methods.

You'll want to become acquainted with the contents of this book well before utilizing the games in any training session, as it will give you an excellent working knowledge of how the brain functions. In so doing, you'll be better equipped to enhance the learning environment by expanding your learners' experience and development through innovative brain-based approaches.

Suggestions for Using Games

Before selecting an activity for your event or program, make sure you have identified the general (or specific) objective or purpose for conducting your game. Become completely familiar with the game and even try it out with some coworkers to make sure you are well prepared to use it in your programs.

Even though all the games in this book have been used successfully with a variety of groups—from entry-level hires to CEOs—it is imperative you establish your own comfort zones in advance.

When you introduce a game, give your attendees a brief explanation of what they'll be experiencing and clearly describe the objectives. Although you may still encounter an occasional indifferent attitude on the part of an attendee, experience has shown that once these individuals understand that it's just not a "game" but a proven way to strengthen and fortify the point you are making, they tend to become actively (and willingly) involved.

While most of these activities require a relatively brief period of time to complete, make sure you always allow sufficient time to debrief the activity and discuss the questions posed. Don't be confined or constrained by the suggested questions; rather, let the group continue their own discussions as needed and appropriate.

Also be aware, however, that this discussion time is not a "gripe session" or time to find axes to grind. As you wander among the groups during their respective discussions, listen carefully to ensure they're on target with their comments and focusing their discussions on the questions at hand. When leading these discussions, be aware of all your participants and try to get everyone involved. You may encounter an occasional "know-it-all" who thinks he or she has all the answers. While it is good to get this person's input, don't let any one individual monopolize the conversations. If you're posting the group's responses on a flip chart, let that person do the recording for the group.

On the other hand, if you find someone who seems reticent to offer *any* comments, make it a point to ask that person a rather easy question. Merely letting him or her give a correct response may supply the confidence needed to take a more active role.

Selecting the Proper Game

As you read through this book, you will find a selection of games/activities at the end of each chapter. While these games may address specific aspects of brain function, such as male versus female brains or the differences between left and right brains, many of them are appropriate for other uses as well.

For example, the activities on creativity are multipurpose and can easily be used in other types of programs. The same is true for some climate-setting activities and those that emphasize strategies for dealing with change.

While all of these games are completely appropriate for small-group workshops (up to 50 participants), many are also usable for large-group keynotes. However, since most keynotes run an hour or less, if this is the nature of your use, select an activity that can be conducted in just a few minutes. The main challenge in using games in keynotes is not getting people to talk—it's how to get them to stop talking when time is up!

This book can be an excellent resource for you in your role as meeting planner, speaker, trainer, or manager.

So let's get to it!

The Use of Games and Activities in the World of Meetings

When I give a lecture, I accept that people look at their watches, but what I do not tolerate is when they look at it and raise it to their ear to find out if it stopped.

—Marcel Achard

Chapter Highlights

In this opening chapter, you will learn several ways to make your meetings more effective. You'll also discover some of the dos and don'ts for using games in meetings.

Ask anyone who has been around the meetings or training arena for a while, and they'll likely all agree on two things when it comes to experiential learning:

1. **Today's meeting and conference attendees want to be entertained as well as be informed. In short, they want proof that learning can be fun.** This is not to say that all learning must be "fun and games," but given the admittedly short attention span of most audiences, it is clear that we must engage and involve our attendees as much as possible. In fact, recent brain research clearly indicates that if we don't in some way engage participants every five to seven minutes, we'll lose them. Additional findings in this area tell us that when we physically move around, the body produces chemicals that have a positive effect on our thinking. Finally, according to the Center for Accelerated Learning, "people who learn in a fun, active way learn faster and remember more." This study also suggested that we can reduce training time by as much as 60 percent owing to this faster absorption.

2. **Learning is not a spectator sport!** Let's think about that for a moment. While we, of course, believe that the content and material we bring to our audiences is relevant, timely, and useful, we're also suggesting that the more they can discuss, debate, and deliberate this information, the more it will resonate with them. It is also true that we often learn as much, if not more, from our colleagues during break times, hallway conversations, and other casual moments we spend conversing with other participants. In other words, the personal experiences we often share with fellow attendees are also a learning activity.

Let's Look at Meetings

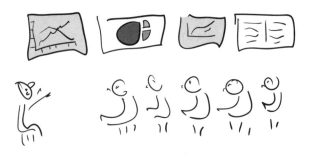

Someone once quipped that if everyone attending a meeting at this very moment were all laid end to end, they'd probably be a lot more comfortable! This would be funny if it weren't so often true. But one look at your own corporate or association meetings is all you need to know he had a point.

Every day literally millions of meetings are held, yet many—perhaps most—fail to hit their mark. Ask any experienced meeting professional, and each one will stress the importance of having goals and objectives for any meeting. Check your own organization's track record, however, and you'll see a different story. For example, an association may have its annual conference each year. And why? you ask. "Well, because we *always* have our annual meeting every year." Sound a bit redundant?

In today's marketplace, with an uncertain economy and continued scrutiny on the entire world of meetings, we'd best be prepared for some serious questions—perhaps even from our superiors, stakeholders, and colleagues.

So, with this brief background, let's look at some tested tips and questions that must be addressed.

Time-Tested Tips for Better Meetings

These suggestions will help ensure that your meetings—from small-group training workshops and seminars to multithousand-attendee conferences or conventions—will all be productive and cost-effective.

Define Your Objectives
- To introduce new information?
- To announce a change?
- To review or modify policies?
- To solve a problem?
- To motivate or reward?
- To introduce a new product?

Do you have a specific goal in mind that others are aware of? If not, why not?

Target Your Outcomes
- What will happen after the meeting is over?
- What are the desired end results of this meeting?
- How will you know if these end results are met?
- How will your manager or the participants know if results are met?

In many associations, we have seen a strong trend whereby potential speakers and facilitators are required to identify, prior to speaking, three or four solid takeaways or outcomes that their participants can expect to learn.

In the old days, an objective could be simply "to understand" or "to appreciate" a certain concept; clearly, that language won't cut it today. Experienced meeting professionals are demanding these objectives in action-oriented, behavioral terms, such as "to identify the five steps in closing a sale" or to "demonstrate at least three ways to increase customer satisfaction."

Define Your Participants
- Who will be coming to your meeting? Are these the appropriate people?
- Do they have sufficient experience or background to be able to contribute to the meeting's goals?
- Do you know what their expectations are? Might there be some hidden agenda items on their minds?
- Can you be sure they'll be listening to you, rather than texting or using their BlackBerrys the whole time?
- Are they there because they really want to be there—or is it a case of a captive audience (i.e., "I'm here because my boss told me I had to come")?

Determine the Agenda
- What are the topics that should be covered?
- For small group meetings, do you have a prepared agenda?

- Will your participants have the agenda in advance?
- Will attendees have an opportunity to make changes or suggestions to the agenda? Can you be flexible enough to allow them to do so?

Consider Timing

- How long will the meeting last?
- What time of day is it scheduled for?
- Has sufficient time been allowed to adequately cover all the necessary items? If not, when will the next meeting be scheduled?
- What day(s) of the week? For example, Mondays or Fridays are often not the best days for meetings, because people's energy levels are best in the middle of the week. Meetings are usually most successful when held on Tuesdays or Wednesdays.

Define Roles

- What roles and responsibilities will the attendees have?
- Will you need a facilitator? Timekeeper? Scribe? Parliamentarian?
- Are the attendees comfortable in their assignments? Have they volunteered themselves, or have they *been* volunteered by a third party?

Decide on Process or Method

- Do the items on the agenda call for decisions, or are they merely informational?
- If your role is that of a facilitator, have you ensured that everyone will have a chance to participate?
- If yours is a training or speaking assignment, have you allowed time for interaction or other ways of engaging or involving the group?

Identify Action Steps

- As the meeting closes, have you identified the action steps the group has agreed on?
- Does everyone have marching orders?
- Have you made a "to do" list to ensure that nothing was left undone?

Nothing is quite as perplexing or frustrating to a group as leaving a meeting with no clear idea of what is going to happen next. The attendees are likely to feel their time has been wasted.

Evaluate the Meeting

- After the meeting, have you informed participants and other relevant parties of the actions and decisions made?
- In retrospect, were the right decisions made? If not, what needs to be done next?

Certainly a formal evaluation or critique is an expected part of any training program, but even in small-group get-togethers some type of follow-up is of paramount importance.

Now then . . .

Characteristics of Games and Activities

With that brief look at the world of meetings under our belts, let's turn our attention to some traits of these learning activities. Essentially, a game or exercise can be used to support and enhance the learning point or content you are presenting. Whether you're offering cognitive, affective, or psychomotor types of learning, all three can be reinforced through the use of audience involvement activities.

It is important to remember, of course, that the game is not the focal point of the learning—it is used to embellish and support the learning. In short, don't let the adage of "the tail wagging the dog" come into play.

In this book, you will find these characteristics in all the activities presented:

- **Brief:** In most cases, these activities range in duration from a few minutes to 20 or 30. While we all have seen some activities that take an hour or longer, we strongly believe that the shorter, the better. This is merely to suggest that people want content, and while games are, of course, fun, they must take a secondary role to the information being presented.
- **Low risk:** All of the exercises presented here have been used with groups around the globe. All have been field-tested with a variety of groups, from entry level to executive levels, and given the proper time for processing, you can be assured they will work for you as well.
- **Adaptable:** Regardless of the groups with whom you are working, use the games as presented here or, better yet, tailor them more to the particular audience.

- **Inexpensive:** As you will note, most of the games require very little if any other resources. Even with those that suggest handouts, in the spirit of "going green," these can easily be transferred to PowerPoint slides.
- **Targeted:** Most games will have a specific objective or learning point. However, you may find other tangential uses for them as well. If so, so much the better. Read through the selected exercises and make your judgment accordingly.

Suggestions for the Use of Games

Recent brain research shows the importance of both mental and physical activity to enhance memory and the learning process. So keep these points in mind as you plan and orchestrate your next program.

In summary, consider these suggestions for optimal results with the use of these games:

- **Be prepared.** It's been said that the three most important parts of any presentation are (1) preparation, (2) preparation, and, of course, (3) preparation! It's also been joked that "preparation makes up for a lack of talent." We wouldn't say so, of course, but the underlying point holds up: plan and practice the game with coworkers, family, or friends. This will give you a solid comfort zone and better prepare you for any situation.
- **Be brief.** As already stated, make your point and move on. And remember, the games are always an added benefit, a fun way of imparting information. Don't let them be the main course. Certainly, a two- or three-minute get-acquainted activity at the beginning of a small-group get-together is a must (especially if the attendees don't know one another), but don't use too many too early. Here are a few rules of thumb: In a 45-minute keynote, use maybe two or three games at most. In a half-day or longer workshop, sprinkle several throughout the day. Sometimes all that's needed is a quick break to stand up and move around.
- **Be purposeful.** The old saying "You can't get lost if you don't know where you're going" may well be true, but it has no value in today's

workplace. Each of the games herein has a specific goal or objective, clearly stated below the game's title. Certainly, you may find additional purposes as well. This is fine, but always make certain that your participants know your precise reason or objective for any game or activity. Always allow sufficient time to debrief the activity. This processing time is most valuable in that it allows all your participants to better understand the goal and how that exercise added to the point you were making.

- **Seek participation.** This may sound trite, but if you want the involvement of the group, you'd best demonstrate that you can have fun too. Acknowledge openly that you may not have all the answers but are honestly soliciting attendees' assistance and participation in making this particular program all the more viable and rewarding for them. Games exist to help facilitate learning, and for many people learning is a self-developmental process. Moreover, given the nature of today's audiences, their attention won't necessarily be on their speaker or facilitator 100 percent of the time. Clearly no one wants to be "talked at" today, and by getting them involved, you're already on your way to a more productive and enjoyable workshop.

- **Be playful.** This doesn't mean act like a stand-up comedian, but rather that it's OK to have some fun in your sessions. By letting people know this at the beginning of your program, you're already well on the way to establishing the rapport so critical with any group. Keep in mind, of course, that games have a place in most—but not necessarily all—programs. There are times when overt humor would be clearly inappropriate. But that doesn't mean that you still can't have audience involvement along the way.

Some Caveats

While our bias for group participation is a serious one, we'd be remiss if we didn't mention just a few things to watch out for along the way.

- **Don't be gimmicky.** If you're seen as the "class clown," you're in the wrong business! And if your program comes off as nothing but fun and games, then you are *really* in the wrong business. As you go through this book, you will see dozens of activities that are fun and enjoyable; but make certain that you always emphasize the objective and learning points. The last thing you want is to have your participants walk away with these questions unanswered: What was I supposed to learn? Was that time really worth the effort? What was his point? Why did she spend so much time playing that game?

- **Don't overdo it.** As previously mentioned, the game is always an appetizer or dessert, but not the main part of the meal. Use the game at—and only at—the appropriate time. And remember, it doesn't always have to be a playful game. The activity could take many forms, as long as it's relevant and ties into the point being made.

- **Don't use games to kill time.** Time is a more precious commodity now than ever, and your attendees' time is far too valuable to waste. Choose your activity wisely—if a point can be made with a 10-minute exercise, why spend 30 minutes achieving the same goal?

- **Avoid the "hardening" of the categories.** These presentation topics tend to be fairly fluid. Be innovative; be creative. Find alternative uses for the games presented. Add, delete, or change these items as you see fit. By mixing it up, you will ensure that your audiences are with you all the way!

That's it. Ladies and gentlemen, start your engines!

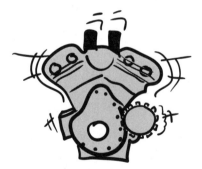

Brain Teaser #1

Materials

Copy of the Brain Teaser #1 handout (provided) for each attendee

Time

5 to 15 minutes

Procedure

Give each audience member a copy of the handout. Explain that each of the 16 frames or boxes in the quiz suggests a well-known slogan, phrase, or saying and that the task is to decipher the hidden message in each box. To get the ball rolling and ensure that the group has a clear understanding of how the quiz works, provide the answer to one of the frames.

Allow participants two to three minutes to do the quiz individually. Then suggest that they pair up with a partner and see how many more frames they can solve together. Allow another two to three minutes. Then, starting with frame #1, begin soliciting answers from the group. If a response is fairly close to the "right" answer (if they've got the idea but perhaps a word wrong), simply paraphrase the answer to make it the correct one.

Discussion Questions

1. How many frames were you able to solve correctly on your own?
2. How many more did you solve when you worked with others?
3. When working with partners, did you come up with alternate answers?
4. Are you able to create some of these brain teasers yourself? Try one now. Is it easier solving a brain teaser or creating a brain teaser?

Brain Teaser #1

Decipher the hidden meaning of each box. Each of these describes a well-known saying or slogan.

1. DEEF	**2.** AZILAKWI	**3.** Doing Learn	**4.** L O A D
5. GAIN GAIN GAIN	**6.** APPLE ⌐	**7.** CH ATTE	**8.** TORIAL TORIAL
9. TREHIDASURE	**10.** LONELY	**11.** S H E E T	**12.** BA NK
13. BJAOCKX	**14.** AgNNIVERSARY	**15.** BUЯ	**16.** CONDU

Brain Teaser #1 Answers

1. Feedback

2. United States

3. Learn by doing

4. Upload

5. Capital gains

6. Apple cider

7. Endless chatter

8. Tutorials

9. Hidden treasure

10. Lonely at the top

11. Spreadsheet

12. Break the bank

13. Jack in the box

14. Silver anniversary

15. Rub the wrong way

16. Semiconductor

Brainstorming

Materials

Paper clips, paper, pencils

Time

5 to 10 minutes

Procedure

Explain that the brain works 24/7 and that research has shown that every 90 minutes there is a literal "storming" of the brain; hence the term *brainstorming*.

Before you delve into a real-world problem—how to increase productivity, how to decrease costs, how your company can become more green, and the like—you'll want to acclimate the group to this process with a trial run. Ask the participants to form teams of three or four members. Explain that their task is to think of as many uses as they can for a common paper clip, in just two minutes. Ask them to jot down only the number of ideas—not the ideas themselves. Encourage a fun, competitive atmosphere.

First review the rules for brainstorming:

1. No critical judgment is allowed.
2. Freewheeling is welcomed—the wilder, the better!
3. Quantity, not quality, is desired—the more, the merrier!
4. Recombination and improvement are sought.

Variation

As an alternate activity, ask "How would you improve the common lead pencil?"

Discussion Questions

1. How many ideas did your team generate?
2. What are some of the uses you thought of? (tie clasp, make a chain, etc.)
3. What are some of the more outlandish ideas you thought of?
4. Did you find the group-think process brought forth more ideas?

Creative People
I Have Known

OBJECTIVE

- To show that creativity is not confined to well-known artists and celebrities

Materials

Pens, paper

Time

10 to 15 minutes

Procedure

Ask the group to form teams of two to three. Ask that they begin by writing down, as fast as they can, as many words or terms associated with characteristics of creativity, originality, imagination, ingenuity, or inventiveness as they can think of. After three or four minutes, ask teams to share some of their findings. Now ask them to record the names of people they have known—coworkers and colleagues, relatives, managers, friends, etc.—who have really shown creativity in their work or their lives. You want them to realize that we are surrounded every day by originality, imagination, and ingenuity. Throw modesty to the wind and suggest they can even talk about themselves.

Discussion Questions

1. Did teammates mention characteristics that you hadn't considered creative traits?
2. As you recorded the creative people in your life, why did their names come to your minds?
3. What are the traits they've shown to express creativity?
4. Is there a common thread running through the list of creative people, such as age, gender, or type of work? Are the traits discussed transferrable?
5. What traits do you personally find most inspiring?

Six Thinking Hats (Group Perspective)

OBJECTIVE

- To demonstrate how our creative thinking abilities can enhance and expand the quality of our decision-making process

Materials

Copies of the Six Thinking Hats description (provided), paper, pens

Time

20 to 30 minutes

Procedure

Dr. Edward de Bono, recognized as one of the gurus of creative thinking, proposed a novel way of increasing our power of lateral thinking. In his book *The Six Thinking Hats*, he describes a process that affords us the opportunity to explore and better understand the complexity of a concept, idea, or decision by looking at it from different points of view. Metaphorically, each of the different-colored hats represents a different thinking approach, style, or perspective that we each possess, consciously or unconsciously.

Divide participants into five teams (explain that only five teams are necessary since you, as the leader, will be wearing the blue hat) and randomly assign the other five hat colors to the teams. Come to agreement on a current, central, or significant idea, concept, or decision you wish to work on. (You may already have established a topic that is relevant or even critical to the purpose of today's meeting .) Distribute copies of the "Six Thinking Hats" description or display it on a PowerPoint slide. Review with the participants the different styles of thinking. Request that the members of each team, while "wearing" their assigned hat and responding in accordance with that thinking style, discuss and record their responses to the topic at hand. (These findings will be in the form of questions, answers, suggestions, facts, feelings, or criticisms—depending on which hat is being worn). After 5 to 15 minutes (depending on the complexity of the topic), ask the teams to share their findings.

Discussion Questions

1. Teams—From the perspective of your assigned hat color, what are your findings on the topic posed? (Ask each of the five teams.)
2. Would you have felt more comfortable responding from a different hat color— a different perspective or style? If so, why?
3. Do you know some people who wear the same hat all the time?
4. Do you now have a different or varied perspective concerning the topic?
5. Can you see how considering a question from various thinking styles could be helpful in other areas or with other topics?

Six Thinking Hats

Metaphorically, each of the different-colored hats represents a different thinking approach, state, or perspective. Asking all these questions can improve the quality of our decision making.

- **Green Hat** (Creative Thinking): no criticism; just creativity. Explore, investigate, and expand your idea, decision, or concept and, in so doing, give way to freewheeling thinking.
- **Red Hat** (Feeling): What is your gut-level reaction or instinctive feeling (not your justification—just your emotional response)? Are you passionate, fearful, or uncertain about this idea?
- **White Hat** (Neutrality): Like the color white, this approach stresses neutrality. Be objective; list the pros and cons, using only the facts you have. Look for cracks or holes in your theory and address them with the appropriate data.
- **Black Hat** (Negative Judgment): This is the caution flag. Play the devil's advocate; list reasons this idea may not be the best after all. What are some objections? Why should you be cautious?
- **Yellow Hat** (Positive Judgment): Be optimistic and sunny about this idea. What are all the possible benefits and the value of this decision or idea?
- **Blue Hat** (Process Control): This hat is worn by the meeting's chairperson(s). Like directing traffic, the blue hat helps to facilitate the discussion and debate. (You may suggest revisiting a team's response if new information merits it or inviting teams to question each other.)

Six Thinking Hats (Individual Perspective)

OBJECTIVE

- To demonstrate how our creative thinking abilities can enhance and expand the quality of our decision-making process

Materials

Copies of the Six Thinking Hats handout (provided), paper, pens

Time

20 to 30 minutes

Procedure

Dr. Edward de Bono, recognized as one of the "gurus" of creative thinking, proposed a novel way of increasing our power of lateral thinking. In his book *The Six Thinking Hats*, he describes a process that affords us the opportunity to explore and better understand the complexity of a concept, idea, or decision by looking at it from different points of view. Metaphorically, each of the different-colored hats represents a different thinking approach, style, or perspective that we each possess, consciously or unconsciously.

Explain to participants that they will have an opportunity to look more closely at a current challenge (an idea, concept, proposal, or decision) and explore it from different thinking perspectives to improve the quality of their decision making.

Distribute copies of the Six Thinking Hats handout or display it on a PowerPoint slide. Review with the participants the different styles of thinking "hats."

Explain that they will be recording their idea, concept, or proposal at the top of the handout and then using the different thinking approaches (represented by the hats) to explore their idea. Allow 10 minutes for this individual work and then ask participants to find a partner to assist in expanding their approach. Allow another 5 minutes for this interaction.

Discussion Questions

1. Did you become aware of other ideas, questions, or options based on the "hat" approach?

2. Is there a particular hat-color approach that you feel more comfortable working from?

3. Do you know some people who wear the same hat all the time?

4. Do you now have a different or varied perspective concerning your topic?

5. Can you see how this approach—using different thinking styles—could be helpful in other areas or with other topics?

Six Thinking Hats

Metaphorically, each of the different-colored hats represents a different thinking approach, state, or perspective. Asking all these questions can improve the quality of our decision making.

Write your idea, proposal, or decision:

_____

_____

Read the following "hat" descriptions and jot down any idea that would materially assist you in exploring your concept.

- **Green Hat** (Creative Thinking): no criticism; just creativity. Explore, investigate, and expand your idea, decision, or concept and, in so doing, give way to freewheeling thinking.

_____

_____

- **Red Hat** (Feeling): What is your gut-level reaction or instinctive feeling (not your justification—just your emotional response)? Are you passionate, fearful, or uncertain about this idea?

_____

_____

- **White Hat** (Neutrality): Like the color white, this approach stresses neutrality. Be objective; list the pros and cons, using only the facts you have. Look for cracks or holes in your theory and address them with the appropriate data.

_____

_____

- **Black Hat** (Negative Judgment): This is the caution flag. Play the devil's advocate; list reasons this idea may not be the best after all. What are some objections? Why should you be cautious?

  _____

  _____

- **Yellow Hat** (Positive Judgment): Be optimistic and sunny about this idea. What are all the possible benefits and the value of this decision or idea?

  _____

  _____

- **Blue Hat** (Process Control): Like directing traffic, the Blue Hat helps to facilitate discussion and debate and points to the next step in the process.

  _____

  _____

Who's on First?

OBJECTIVE
- To practice logic and problem-solving skills

Materials

Copies of the Who's on First? handout and Organizational Chart handout (provided)

Time

15 to 20 minutes

Procedure

Tell the group they will be working in teams of two or three to identify personnel on an organization chart. Suggest that, while on the surface they don't appear to have enough information to solve the problem, in fact they do. Advise them to use their logic, deductive thinking, and a process of elimination to make the solution easier to arrive at.

Tip

If you see some groups are having difficulty getting started, suggest they draw a matrix and simply use this process of elimination.

Discussion Questions

1. How many of us almost gave up from the start? Why?

2. Did anyone use a matrix approach in working this out?

3. How often at work are we faced with problems that seem unsolvable?

4. How do you react when a problem seems unsolvable?

Who's on First?

As you study the following bits of information, determine which individuals fill the respective roles in this hotel's organization chart. Write their names in the appropriate place on the organizational chart provided.

Hotel Personnel

Ms. A. Wood

Mr. C. Quin

Mr. S. Silva

Miss P. Wagner

Miss T. Thain

Mr. B. Stephen

Facts to Consider

1. The general manager's grandson is the assistant manager.

2. The front desk manager's son-in-law is the food and beverage manager.

3. Mr. Stephen has never had children.

4. Mr. Silva is 23 years of age.

5. The administrative assistant's first cousin is Miss Thain.

6. The general manager lives next door to Mr. Quin.

7. Miss Wagner and Miss Thain celebrated their twenty-fifth birthdays last week.

Organizational Chart

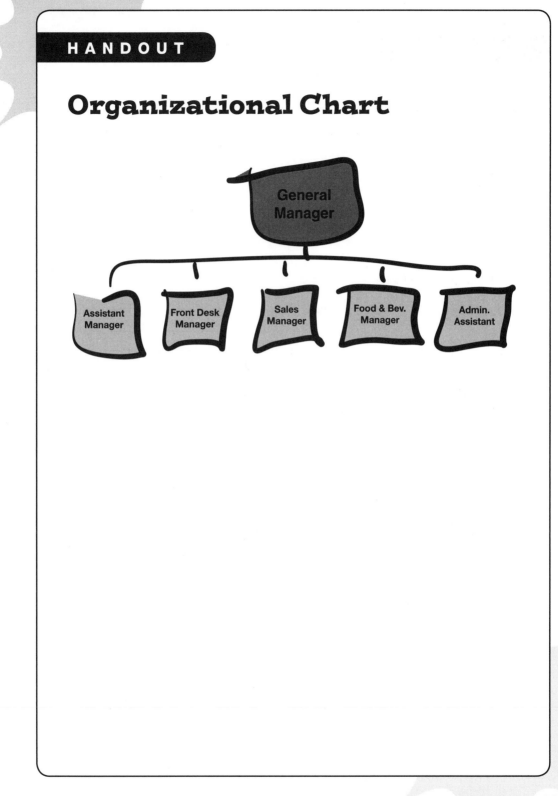

Who's on First? Answers

General Manager: Ms. Wood

Assistant Manager: Mr. Stephen

Front Desk Manager: Mr. Quin

Sales Manager: Miss Thain

Food and Beverage Manager: Mr. Silva

Administrative Assistant: Miss Wagner

The fastest and easiest way to solve this problem is to use a matrix and a process of elimination.

Each of the pieces of information gives important clues as to where each individual fits into the organization chart.

For example:

1. *The hotel's general manager's grandson is the assistant manager.* This tells us that the assistant manager is male, thereby eliminating Ms. Wood, Miss Wagner, and Miss Thain. Further, it suggests that Mr. Stephen, never having had children, could not be the general manager, and Mr. Silva, at 23, is too young to have a grandchild.

2. *The front desk manager's son-in-law is the food and beverage manager.* This quickly eliminates the three women as the food and beverage manager. It also eliminates both Mr. Stephen (no children) and Mr. Silva (too young). With these five out of the running, the only person left is Mr. Quin, who must be the front desk manager.

3. *Mr. Stephen has never had children.* He can't be the front desk manager or the general manager since both people in those postions have had children.

4. *Mr. Silva is 23 years old.* Too young to have a son-in-law, so he can't be the front desk manager.

5. *Miss Thain is the administrative assistant's cousin.* All this tells us is that Ms. Thain is not the administrative assistant.

6. *Mr. Quin lives next door to the general manager.* Obviously, then, he can't be the general manager.

7. *Miss Wagner and Miss Thain celebrated their twenty-fifth birthdays last week.* They are too young to have grown children and therefore cannot be the general manager or the front desk manager.

2

Brain "Very" Basics: What Does It Look Like?

Use it and get more of it.

—Dr. Elkhonon Goldberg, neuropsychologist

Chapter Highlights

This chapter introduces the "very" basics of the major brain structures and their various functions, especially as they relate to the learner.

In the past few years, the public seems to have developed an insatiable appetite for learning more about the human brain. Even the media have jumped on the bandwagon. We continually see news stories on the latest discoveries about this seemingly esoteric "gray matter." No longer the domain of only the academic and neuroscience community, how the brain operates and how we can better nurture and strengthen this prized organ is something we are all invited to join in exploring.

Until approximately 25 years ago, without the advantage of safe, noninvasive technology, researchers found themselves with a daunting and perilous challenge if they attempted to map the inner workings of the healthy human brain. Our knowledge of how the healthy brain functioned was based only on observing how it *malfunctioned*—research was performed mainly on diseased, dysfunctional, and injured brains or the brains of the deceased.

The advent of new brain imaging technologies and other cutting-edge research techniques has allowed researchers to perform much more comprehensive studies of the brain. For example:

- *CAT: Computerized axial tomography* captures multiple x-ray pictures, allowing the view of a full brain image, but does not depict movement.
- *PET: Positron emission tomography* incorporates the use of radioactive particles injected into the brain and monitored as they travel with the blood flow of the brain.
- *SPECT: Single-photon emission-computed tomography*, not unlike the PET, uses radioactive particles to monitor the blood flow in tissue.
- *MRI: Magnetic resonance imaging* provides a 3-D, structural image of the brain, allowing researchers to observe which areas of the brain are activated when a subject performs particular tasks.
- *PET/CT: Positron emission tomography/computerized tomography* combines the advantages of both the PET and the CAT.

- *PEPSI: Proton echo-planar spectroscopic imaging* charts brain chemical activity.
- *MEG: Magnetoencephalography* retrieves information relative to the brain's neuron-firing activity.

These brain image technologies enable our neuroscientists to make great strides in unearthing the mysteries of the human brain; yet most brain specialists will admit that we still know precious little about this amazing organ. One thing's for sure—whatever information our neuroscientists *do* discover is now coveted and shared widely with those in related and nonrelated disciplines, including anthropology, education, linguistics, and psychology.

And it isn't just the scientific and professional communities expressing enthusiasm over the latest brain breakthroughs. The brain-savvy general public also eagerly awaits these findings. The societal trend toward understanding and caring for our bodies (the fitness revolution) has now expanded to include the care and feeding of our brains. Many eminent brain specialists (such as Bruce Lipton, John Medina, Jill Bolte Taylor, Daniel Amen, Louann Brizendine, Richard Restak, Norman Doidge, Sharon Begley, John Demos, and Paul Swingle) have offered up numerous books, CDs, videos, and games on brain function, in easy-to-understand language aimed directly at the lay audience. These exciting developments represent a new era of individuals using brain science to take responsibility for their own mental fitness—*a brain-new world*.

Basic Structure of the Brain

As a trainer, educator, speaker, or leader, it's a good idea for you to have a grasp of a few of the physiological tools that your learners and audience members possess. This information will serve as the foundation for understanding how learners use their brain tools in the acquisition of materials you present.

Understanding the basic biological processes, structures, and functions of the brain is helpful in comprehending critical learning areas such as attention, information processing, consolidating, and memory retrieval. However, knowing the complexity of this topic, we appreciate that even the *basics* may well be overwhelming. Therefore, let's start with the "very" basics.

The brain weighs in at birth at approximately 350 to 400 grams and typically matures to a weight of about 3 pounds in the average adult. It's approximately the size of your two fists pressed together and has been described as having the consistency of firm cottage cheese and the texture of soft tofu. It consists of approximately 78 percent water, 9 percent fat, and 8 percent protein. Size-wise, it comprises only 2 percent of the body's mass but uses 20 to 30 percent of the body's energy. The more active your brain, the more energy it uses (could there be potential here for yet another diet?—*activate your neurons to a slimmer body!*) Safely positioned inside the bony skull, the delicate tissues of the brain enjoy an essential protective encasement. (See Figure 2.1.)

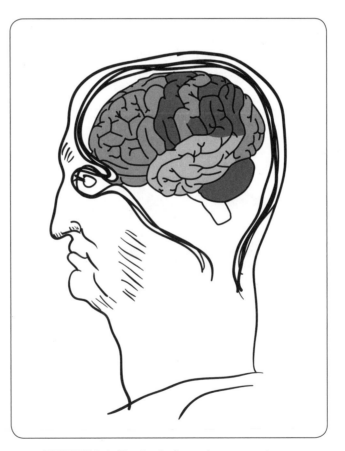

FIGURE 2.1 The brain (based on an anatomy sketch by Leonardo da Vinci)

Let's review the major sections of the brain, starting with the **cerebrum**. The word comes from the Latin for *brain* and is the area that most of us think of when we think of *the brain*—it is where all our thinking, memory, language, speech, and movements are coordinated. Also called "gray matter," it is the largest, most highly developed portion of the brain and, from an evolutionary perspective, the newest part. The cerebrum is divided into symmetric left and right hemispheres, which connect at its base by means of the corpus callosum, which provides a pathway for the two halves to communicate. The left hemisphere controls functions on the right side of the body, and the right hemisphere controls activities on left side of the body. There are functionary differences between the right and left hemispheres of the brain, which scientists term *relative lateralization*. (This does not mean there are right-brained people and left-brained people.) The surface or covering of the cerebrum is called the **cerebrum cortex**. With its 10 billion neurons, the cortex is so highly convoluted that if you took it out of your head and spread it out, it would cover a 2½-square-foot area.

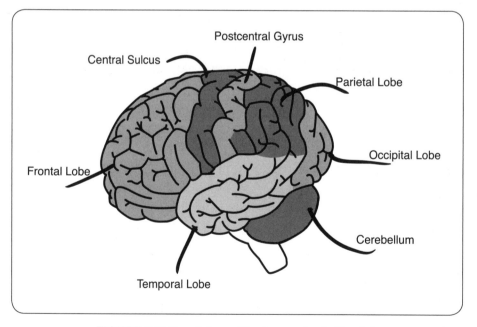

FIGURE 2.2 Four lobes of the human brain (frontal, parietal, temporals, and occipitals)

There are four main areas or regions of the cerebrum, called **lobes** (see Figure 2.2). And although there is some overlap in the functions of the lobes, the following represents the major responsibility of each the sections:

The **frontal lobe,** a term that comes from the Latin word for *forehead*, is responsible for purposeful cognitive activity like speech, creativity, planning, problem solving, judgment, and voluntary movement. Aspects of your personality and your IQ are considered to be governed by processes in the frontal lobe.

The **parietal lobe** is located at the top rear region of the head and processes complex sensory functions like touch, pressure, and perception of the shapes and sizes of objects.

The **temporal lobes** (right and left) are located in the area above the ears. The temporals (the word in Latin means "temple") specialize in hearing, visual, and verbal memory, smell, meaning, and language.

The **occipital lobe** is located in the central back of the head and is predominately responsible for visual reception, shapes, and colors.

Left Brain–Right Brain Specialization

We are whole-brained humans. While it's true that each of the hemispheres specializes in certain areas, these lateralizations are considered only functional trends. Musical awareness is thought to be a right-brain specialization, but musicians will use their left hemisphere to logically assess the tones. Also, if an injury occurs in one hemisphere, it is not uncommon for the other hemisphere to "learn" that function.

There is some evidence suggesting that right- or left-handedness may play a role in the location of specific brain functions. Some studies indicate that in right-handed people the right side of the brain processes spatial information and the left hemisphere processes language; in left-handed individuals it is said to be reversed. However, other studies have found that while 95 percent of right-handed subjects process language in their left hemisphere, only 18 percent of left-handed subjects processed language in their right hemisphere. In addition, their studies revealed that the language function was bilateral in almost 20 percent of the left-handed subjects.

Let's consider the functional trends for the left and right hemisphere:

Left-Brain Specialization	Right-Brain Specialization
Sequencing (lists)	Spatial (maps, puzzles)
Logic	Imagination
Time	Artistic awareness
Analysis	Depth perception
Number skills	Musical activities
Reasoning	Face recognition
Speech	Dreaming
Reading	3-D forms
Writing	Emotional perception
Counting and math	Sense of humor
Symbol recognition	Insight
Processing external stimuli	Processing internal messages

The findings from a recent study directed by Dr. Kazuhiro Shigemoto, Tokyo Metropolitan Institute of Gerontology (2008), may lead to a better understanding of these asymmetrical differences. His team identified structural variations (size, shape, and type of molecular receptors) in the synapses of the right and left hippocampi (seats of memory and learning). Synapses in the right hippocampus were large and complex in shape, with an abundance of one type of glutamate receptors, while synapses in the left hippocampus were small and abundant in another type of receptor. According to Dr. Shigemoto, "This finding may help us understand how our left and right brains work differently."

The **diencephalon** lies at the midline of the brain, beneath the cerebrum and above the brain stem. It includes the thalamus, hypothalamus, epithalamus, subthalamus, pituitary gland, and many other smaller yet significant structures. The thalamus coordinates, somewhat like a relay station, all the incoming sensory information (except smells), while the hypothalamus controls internal body functions, including sleep. The structures within the diencephalon work cooperatively with other areas of the central nervous system, the endocrine system (hormones, growth, metabolism, development), and the limbic system (memory, emotion, behavior, and olfaction). Also located in the diencephalon is the medulla, which controls functions such as sneezing, hiccuping, vomiting, and coughing. You can thank your diencephalon for regulating your sex drive, hunger, thirst, pain, pleasure, stress, blood pressure, and body temperature.

The **brain stem** is located in the lower portion of the brain, connecting the brain with the spinal cord. The brain stem performs the essential life-supporting role of regulating the body's autonomic activities like breathing, heart rate, blood pressure, consciousness, digestion, basic attention, and arousal.

Not unlike the cerebrum, the **cerebellum** consists of two hemispheres but is less than half the size of the cerebrum. It rests in the back of the brain just under the occipital lobe and is attached to the brain stem. It is also known as the "little brain," and with good reason. It comprises only 10 percent of the brain's volume yet supports approximately 50 percent of the brain's neurons. It has been said to function much like a computer and is considered the most complex portion of the brain. Among its many functions, it regulates our balance, posture, and muscle tone and coordinates the sequencing and duration of all our movements. Recent studies support the cerebellum's contribution to many of our cognitive learning processes and emotions and even suggest a mind-body link.

Thus far, two major types of **brain cells** have been discovered. They include neurons (action cells) and glial cells (protector cells). Of the 100 billion brain cells, approximately 10 times more are protector cells than are neurons.

Each neuron expresses its own identity and unique function as it transmits electrochemical signals, carrying out its crucial mission of receiving and transmitting vital information to other neurons. The interneural connections can be vast. Each neuron can transmit up to twenty-five hundred impulses per minute, and its branchlike structures, called *dendrites* (see Figure 2.3) can be connected to some ten thousand other neurons. This translates into a possibility of one quadrillion connections in each person's brain!

The dendrite (signal receiver) accepts a signal and then passes the signal on through its long axon, where it travels to the axon terminal button (signal sender). Here the axon button sends the signal across a gap called the *synaptic gap* to a neighboring dendrite, by mean of chemicals called *neurotransmitters* (Figure 2.4).

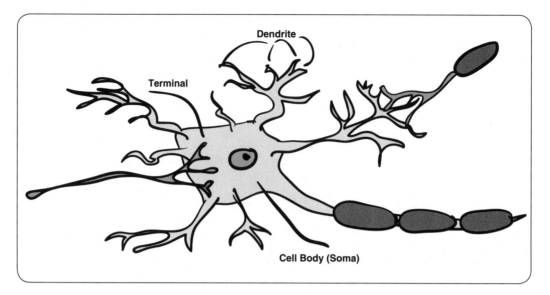

FIGURE 2.3 Dendrite and axon (neurons/brain cells)

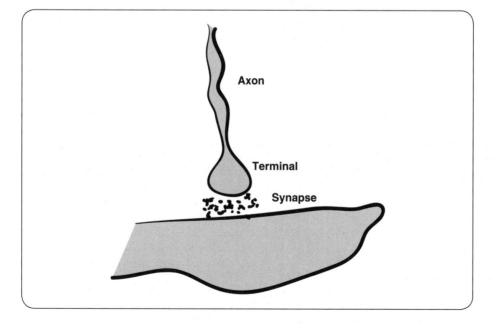

FIGURE 2.4 Synaptic gap and neurotransmitters

The **hippocampus** is located below the cerebrum and above the brain stem and consists of two hippocampi, one on each side of the brain. It belongs to the limbic system, and its curved shape gives it the appearance of a sea horse (*hippocampus* comes from the Greek word for sea monster or sea horse). The hippocampus plays a major role in memory—assisting in the consolidation of learning and converting the stimuli in short-term memory to long-term memory storage. In individuals with Alzheimer's disease, the hippocampus is one of the first regions of the brain to suffer memory damage and disorientation.

Considered a part of the limbic system and attached to the hippocampus, the **amygdala** is a small almond-shaped structure associated with our emotions. In fact, the amygdala's primary role is to form and store memories associated with emotions. The amygdala is not only attached to the hippocampus (involved in learning and memory consolidation) but actively interacts with it. It is believed that the amygdala cooperates in such a way as to link an emotional component to a learned memory. It is not believed that the memory is actually stored in the amygdala, but rather that the emotion is triggered when the memory (which is stored elsewhere) is recalled. The fact that the amygdala is involved in both the sense of smell and emotional memory may well explain why a familiar scent from a past experience can trigger such a strong emotional reaction. Among other functions, the amygdala is also involved with pheromone processing and appetite conditioning.

So as we've seen in this chapter, the brain is a very complex, multifaceted, and elaborately wired organ. Armed with this new knowledge, you can better understand and appreciate the workings of this wondrous marvel! The information introduced in this chapter, while seemingly detailed at times, represents only the basic features of our body's "hard drive." This will serve as a foundation for our explorations, in the following chapters, of attention, memory, and learning.

Disney's Four Cs of Creativity

OBJECTIVE
- To explore four separate dimensions of creativity and how they can be applied personally and professionally

Materials
  None
Time
  10 to 15 minutes

Procedure

The right and left hemispheres of the brain are specialized, designed to process information differently. Creativity is often considered a right-brain specialty, but in fact the process of creativity is so complex that both hemispheres become involved. Walt Disney, perhaps one of the most creative giants ever, suggested that there are four parts (or four Cs) of creativity:

1. Curiosity
2. Courage
3. Confidence
4. Constancy

Ask the group to form teams of two or three and discuss situations that have arisen in their respective positions, where one or more of these traits may have helped or hindered their own attempts at innovation or those of others. Have the members each describe a situation when they have actually used one of these traits to their advantage.

Discussion Questions

1. Have you ever worked in an organization where creativity seemed to be stifled? How did this make you feel?

2. As you recall these experiences now, why do you suppose your superiors acted in this manner?

3. As you discussed your experiences, can you recall a situation when you were given the complete "green light" to show your creativity? What were the results?

All in the Family

OBJECTIVE
- To use both left and right sides of the brain to solve a problem

Materials

Copies of the All in the Family handout (provided)

Time

10 to 15 minutes

Procedure

Pass out copies of the All in the Family handout to each member of the group (or show it on a PowerPoint slide). Suggest that we often face a problem with seemingly insufficient information with which to make a decision. In this activity, read through the facts given and, based on them, use intuition and sound reasoning (inductive and deductive thinking approaches) to identify which of these extended family members are related and tell where they live.

Variation

If time is limited, have the group form teams of three or four to speed up the process.

Discussion Questions

1. Did some of you simply give up, assuming the problem was unsolvable?
2. How did you formulate a strategy to approach this problem?
3. Are you currently facing an issue in which you're not sure you have enough information? How can you proceed?

All in the Family

Beth, Shannon, Cathie, Karen, Mary, and Mike are all friends and members of two different families. Two live in the Phoenix area, two live in the Toronto area, and the others live in the Detroit and Seattle areas.

Your task is to figure out who lives where and how the six are related. Although you are given limited information, by using logic and a process of elimination you can find the answers.

Have fun!

Relevant Facts

1. Karen lives in the western part of the United States and has never been to Canada.

2. Mary and her sister, Cathie, meet for coffee most every day.

3. Shannon and her only sibling, Beth, live in the same country.

4. Cathie lives in the Phoenix area.

5. Mike has three sisters.

Based on this information, fill in the blanks:

Beth lives in _____.

Shannon resides in _____.

Cathie lives in _____.

Karen lives in _____.

Mary lives in her home in _____.

Mike resides in _____.

Who are the members of the two families?

_____   _____

_____   _____

_____   _____

All in the Family Answers

1. Since Karen has not been to Canada, that rules out that area. Further, living in the West rules out Detroit. The fourth clue tells us that Cathie and Mary are in Phoenix—which leaves Seattle as the option for Karen.

2. Mary and Cathie must live in the same general area—i.e., Toronto or Phoenix—thereby ruling out Detroit or Seattle.

3. Since we know that Mary, Karen, and Cathie are from the United States, Shannon and Beth must be from Canada.

4. Since Cathie is in the Phoenix area, she can't be from the other cities.

5. Since Shannon has only one sibling, she and Beth can't be Mike's sisters, so that leaves Mary, Karen, and Cathie from that family and Beth and Shannon from the other family.

Therefore, based on this information:

- Beth and Shannon live in the Toronto area.
- Cathie and Mary live in the Phoenix area.
- Karen lives in Seattle.
- Mike resides in the Detroit area.

The members of the two families are:

- Beth and Shannon
- Mike, Mary, Karen, and Cathie

Wanna Go for a Ride?

OBJECTIVES
- To show the role emotions play in communication
- To show how the brain adapts to changing situations

Materials

Four chairs at the front of the room

Time

5 to 10 minutes

Procedure

This is a fun role-play scenario. Ask for four volunteers to come to the front of the room. Ask one of the four to be seated; he or she will be the bus driver. The other three will be passengers who will "board the bus" one at a time as the bus travels its route. As the first rider takes a chair (gets aboard the bus and takes his or her seat), an audience member shouts out an emotion—"anger," "joy," etc. For the next minute or two, the bus driver and first passenger act out that emotional role in both communication and actions. Then the bus stops, allowing the second passenger to come aboard as another audience member shouts another emotion—"love," "sadness," etc. Then all three (both passengers and the driver) portray that role. Finally, the third passenger is "picked up" as a third emotion is shouted out. Now all four volunteers play out that part.

Discussion Questions

1. How did you (volunteers) feel as you played those roles?
2. Did you really get into the part, or was it difficult to summon?
3. (To group) Have you seen cases where coworkers have played "games" like this—i.e., jumped onto the *emotional bandwagon*?
4. What have you learned about handling these situations?

Take a Letter

OBJECTIVES
- To practice improvisation and spontaneity skills
- To demonstrate how functioning under pressure can be fun

Materials

None

Time

5 to 10 minutes

Procedure

Divide the group into teams of six or seven. Explain to the group members that we use our improvisational talents daily, creating responses in the moment. We improvise words in conversations and improvise solutions to solve problems. Improvisation and spontaneity are a fundamental aspect of our humanness. This exercise is a fun way to both practice your skills of improvisation and encourage the growth of new brain cells—the brain forms new pathways when new and challenging experiences are introduced.

First, explain that the person starting the game will call out the name of an animal. The next person silently identifies the last letter of the animal (e.g., *horse*—the last letter is *e*) and then quickly shouts the name of an animal beginning with the letter *e*—such as *elephant*. The next person shouts out the name of an animal that begins with the letter *t*. The group continues until it runs out of animals to name or runs out of steam—whichever comes first!

Discussion Questions

1. Even though this was a fun activity, did you feel pressured?

2. Under this type of pressure, did you find you listened more carefully?

3. Why is it that people don't listen like this all the time?

4. How do you typically listen under stressful conditions?

One Word at a Time

OBJECTIVES
- To practice improvisation skills
- To demonstrate how functioning under pressure can be fun

Materials

None

Time

5 to 10 minutes

Procedure

Ask for seven or eight volunteers to join you at the front of the room. The audience shouts a question, such as "What is the meaning of life?" The first volunteer begins by responding to the question with the first word and only the first word of the response. For example, he or she might say "The" and then stop. The second person must quickly continue with another word, such as "meaning." Our brains form new pathways when new and challenging experiences are introduced, so putting the volunteers under pressure to continue the sentence is a great exercise. Continue on in sequence until the question is answered. After two or three minutes, ask for another set of volunteers and pose another question. Your questions might be job related if you choose—or not!

Discussion Questions

1. Did you (volunteers) find your listening skills were heightened?
2. Did you really concentrate on the preceding words?
3. (To the entire group) Have you seen situations when people don't really listen but instead go through the motions?
4. What have you learned about handling these situations?

Stand Up–Sit Down

OBJECTIVES
- To gain an understanding of the group dynamics
- To get energized

Materials

None

Time

10 minutes

Procedure

You'll be asking a series of questions that are relevant to the topic at hand, such as "How many of you have been in your present job for fewer than six months?' Ask those to stand if their answer is yes. The others stay seated. Then ask a follow-up question, such as "How many of you have had a mentor at work?" Again, if those who are standing can answer yes, they stay standing. Otherwise, they sit down. If those seated can answer yes, they stand. Continue for three or four minutes.

Other suggested fun questions:

- How many of you have been to Disneyland/Disney World?
- How many of you have teenagers at home?
- How many of you wish you didn't have teenagers at home?
- How many of you have more job responsibilities than last year?
- How many of you are on Facebook?

Encourage the group to formulate and shout out questions of their own as well.

3

Brain Myths: Separating Fact from Fiction

Brain: an apparatus with which we think we think.

—Ambrose Bierce

Chapter Highlights

This chapter provides an overview of five of the more long-standing myths about the brain and its functions.

As we age, we acquire knowledge, gain skills, transform our attitudes, and even finely tune our insights. But along the way we may also unwittingly buy into some incorrect information. When it comes to the brain, outdated research methodologies and equipment have been replaced with improved sampling methods and cutting-edge, noninvasive, innovative technologies. The results of investigative studies in such fields as neuroscience, pharmacology, artificial intelligence, and psychology are now providing the scientific community, the educational arena, and the general public a wealth of new learning—and debunking pervasive myths about the brain that have been held for decades. Here are a few of the most famous Brain Myths.

We Use Only 10 Percent of Our Brain

The 10 percent brain myth has been promoted for roughly a century now. Versions of this myth have been circulated, altered, expanded, and propagated to the point that its origin is unidentifiable. Many who have spread this myth have not done so in a deliberate attempt to be deceptive; rather out of the belief (or perhaps hope) that we humans have many more abilities or capabilities waiting to be tapped.

Here's a scenario that illustrates how we use much more than 10 percent of our brains: You decide to stop by your neighborhood bookstore, where they happen to serve your favorite coffee. Your goal is to check out the most recently published brain game books (couldn't resist!) and to order a latte. A simple task, you say, but let's look closer. Movement and coordination are required as you walk into the store. Movement is accomplished thanks to your *motor cortex* at the back of your frontal lobes, which allows you to consciously move your muscles, and coordination, an ability provided by your *cerebellum*, the second-largest part of your brain, which controls balance and posture. You walk toward the back of the store, and your eyes cast about, hoping you won't see a long line. The recognition and understanding of visual information is processed in your *occipital lobes*, situated toward the back of your brain. Your olfactory senses are alerted by the rich coffee aroma as it drifts toward your nostrils. Smells travel from your nasal cavity to your *olfactory bulbs* into the *limbic system* of your brain. The server recognizes you and asks if you want your regular. Your *temporals* process the sounds of his voice. Also located in your *temporal* lobes is *Wernicke's area*, responsible for understanding language. Thanks to your *Broca's area* in your motor cortex, which is involved in speech production, you are able to respond with an appreciative "Yes, thanks." As you pick up your cup of java, sensory receptors in your skin travel to your *sensory cortex* in your *parietal lobes*, and you feel the warmth of the cup in your hands.

Now, if you remember that this elaborate explanation was for the purpose of demonstrating that we use far more than 10 percent of our brains, you are using your hippocampus, responsible for transferring short-term memory into long-term memory, as well as your *frontal cortex,* which is responsible for retrieving those memories.

Suppose you tripped and fell on the way out of the bookstore, fracturing your skull and suffering brain damage. Can you imagine the doctor excitedly telling you that he has some good news and some bad news—the bad news being that you have brain damage in 90 percent of your brain and the good news that it's in the 90 percent you never use? Of course not. The fact is that you use virtually all parts of your brain, every day. The real question to ask yourself is "What percentage of your *potential* do you use?"

Some People Are Left-Brained; Some People Are Right-Brained

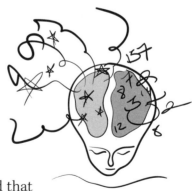

When was the last time someone asked you, "Are you left-brained (logical, linear, deductive, and mathematical) or right-brained (creative, artistic, visual, and imaginative)? This right-brained/left-brained myth likely took root in the 1800s, when it was discovered that damage to one side of the brain often caused a loss of specific abilities. The myth was reinforced by the 1960s Nobel Prize–winning work of Roger Wolcott Sperry on "split-brain" patients. In an effort to decrease the severity of his patients' intractable epilepsy, Dr. Sperry severed his patients' corpus callosum, thus reducing the severity and violence of their epileptic seizures. The corpus callosum (more than two million nerve connections) attaches the two halves and affords a means of communication between them. The results of severing the corpus callosum and its related neural pathways did, indeed, diminish seizure activity in many patients, but it also created a fascinating condition: the two separated hemispheres functioned individually—like two brains in one body. After the connection between the two hemispheres was severed, any new information, experiences acquired, or learning by the left hemisphere was completely unknown to the right hemisphere, and what the right hemisphere learned was completely unknown to the left. With the two hemispheres no longer working in unison, it was as though the individuals functioned with two separate minds—causing, at times, a Jekyll and Hyde effect. Split-brain research continues today to contribute valuable information on hemispheric specialization and integration. An informative, entertaining, interactive game on split-brain research can be found at http://nobelprize.org/educational_games/medicine/split-brain/splitbrain exp.html.

Thankfully, the majority of us have not experienced a hemispherotomy—our corpus callosums are intact, and our two hemispheres are united—continually communicating and cooperating as a seamless whole.

Multitasking Saves Time

In our harried, stressed, "Should have had it done yesterday!" world, we attempt to make the very most of the time we do have, so it seems like a good idea to multitask. Multitasking is the ability to simultaneously focus on and perform two or more tasks. Not possible, say the neuroscientists, who can, in real time, view images within your brain while you are performing specific tasks. Based on these recent studies, it seems that we have no choice but to perform the next cognitive task only after the last one is completed. The brain processes information sequentially, one task at a time; thus, when attempting to focus on more than one thing, the brain is forced to switch from task to task. This switching process may take only milliseconds, but milliseconds could be crucial, depending on the situation (to invoke one of the most dangerous examples, driving and focusing on a stressful phone conversation).

Does your typical day look like this? You're in your office, and you're working on your expense report (task #1) while keeping an eye out for your manager, who is dropping by sometime this afternoon, expecting to pick up another report—which still needs a couple more touches (task #2), and you're monitoring your e-mail screen, watching for your wife's response regarding tonight's change of plans (task #3). Each time you switch your attention from any one of the three tasks to another, not only is valuable time lost, but the potential for mistakes doubles. Then, in addition to your numerous existing tasks, come the uninvited tasks—the interruptions. Dr. John Medina, in his book *Brain Rules*, says, "Studies show that a person who is interrupted takes 50 percent longer to accomplish a task" *and* "makes up to 50 percent more errors." So the next time you're interrupted and claim that it's not a problem because you're such an excellent multitasker, think again! (Which will, of course, require additional switching.)

Drinking Alcohol Kills Brain Cells

Picture this scene: You're a teenager, just home from an exciting socially based peer event (OK, OK, you were out drinking) with alcohol on your breath. Did your parents sit you down and say, "You know, Johnny, you shouldn't drink; you have to be very careful because alcohol kills brain cells"? Most of us probably remember this unfortunate warning. Could it really be true? Could that irresponsible behavior be causing deliberate neural massacre? Could it be severe enough that one would "run out" of brain cells? Granted, even back then evidence showed that we have trillions of brain cells, so one might wonder if, indeed, this tale *were* true. What was the ratio of the amount of alcohol consumed to the number of cells destroyed? When I was a teen, we even discussed this topic in our biology class. How much alcohol could you devour and retain your mental faculties? After all, we wanted a sufficient number of brain cells left to get into college—at the very least!

How relieved we would have been to know it was a myth! Drinking alcohol *does not* kill brain cells.

But don't be too eager to celebrate. Drinking alcohol may not kill brain cells, but in excess it can cause injury to your cells' dendrites, thereby damaging your cells' communication pathways. It seems alcohol can destroy the end branches of nerve cells, slowing intercellular communication and disrupting vital brain functions such as new cell growth. This disruption of new cellular growth is suspected to cause long-term deficits in the hippocampi (seat of long-term memory) of moderate to heavy drinkers. Reversal of cell damage is possible when alcohol is restricted, but this repair process is not always total.

Still, there are some doctors who are not totally antialcohol, as long as it's consumed in moderation. When a medical professional uses the word *moderate* with regard to alcohol consumption, how much does that mean? Dr. Andrew Weil suggests that moderate drinking, at least for those under the age of 65, is no more than one drink a day for women and no more than two drinks a day for men. We'll drink to that!

You Can't Grow New Brain Cells

Up until the late 1980s it was believed that we could grow new cells in other parts of our body but not in the brain. Essentially, that meant we are born with a finite number of neurons and that is it—for life. So, it was deemed, if cells in your brain died (which they regularly do) or were damaged or destroyed through brain injury, you'd simply have to endure a neuron scarcity for the rest of your life.

Then came the welcome discovery that adult humans are the proud possessors of a process call *neurogenesis*. Neurogenesis (meaning "birth of neurons") is responsible for new neuron growth not only in prenatal stages of development but also throughout adulthood. It seems the most prominent area of neurogenesis is in the hippocampus, the center for memory and learning.

Would you like to increase neurogenesis in your brain? Get more exercise and decrease your stress levels, and you'll be well on your way to celebrating the birth of your delicate new little neurons.

Fact or Fiction?

In all likelihood, you found a surprise or two among these myths and misconceptions. But don't blame yourself—when we hear something over and over, especially from trusted authorities (like parents!), we naturally believe it.

But now you know better! Go forth and spread the word.

Brain Teaser #2

OBJECTIVES
- To do something "just for fun"
- To practice creativity and creative problem solving

Materials

Copy of the Brain Teaser #2 handout (provided) for each attendee

Time

5 to 15 minutes

Procedure

Give each audience member a copy of the handout. Explain that each of the 16 frames or boxes in the quiz suggests a well-known slogan, phrase, or saying and that the task is to decipher the hidden message in each box. To ensure that the group has a clear understanding of how the quiz works, provide the answer to one of the frames. Allow participants two to three minutes to do the quiz individually. Then suggest that they pair up with a partner and see how many more frames they can solve together. Allow another two to three minutes. Then, starting with frame #1, begin soliciting answers from the group. If a response is fairly close to the "right" answer, simply paraphrase the answer to make it the correct one.

Discussion Questions

1. How many frames were you able to solve correctly on your own?
2. How many more did you solve when you worked with others?
3. When working with partners, did you come up with alternate answers?
4. Are you able to create some of these brain teasers yourself? Try one now. Is it easier solving a brain teaser or creating a brain teaser?

Brain Teaser #2

Decipher the hidden meaning of each box. Each of these describes a well-known saying or slogan.

1.
 	
  B   R
   N
   I   A
	2.
	
	SITTING
	WORLD
		3.
		L H
		A T
		U E
		G R
			4.
			ESTHOLDEEM

5. TOMORROWDAY	**6.** JUST + H$_2$O	**7.** EILN PU	**8.** TIME TI
9. MY MIN . . .	**10.** TRAVELING CCCCCCCCCC	**11.** N I A C	**12.** FORK $$$$$$$$

13.
 	
• That that
	14.
	
	FLOWAT
		15.
		
		IFLAND IFIFC
			16.
			
			  R
			R E D
			  D

Brain Teaser #2 Answers

1. Scatterbrain

2. Sitting on top of the world

3. Side-splitting laughter

4. Hold in high esteem

5. Day after tomorrow

6. Just add water

7. Line up in alphabetical order

8. Time and a half

9. My mind went blank

10. Traveling overseas

11. Raising Cain

12. Fork over the money

13. That's beside the point

14. Low in fat

15. One if by land, two if by sea

16. Red Cross

You Can't Teach an Old Dog . . .

Materials

None

Time

15 to 20 minutes

Procedure

Explain to your participants that until the late 1980s it was believed we could not grow new brain cells. Of course, we now know that to be false. Neurogenesis (the birth of nerve cells) is responsible for new neuron growth throughout life, and the most prominent area of this growth takes place in the brain's hippocampus, the center for memory and learning.

We have also become aware that some aspects of brain function actually increase with age; we become mellower and wiser. Many individuals have come into their own during later stages of life. For example, Colonel Sanders started Kentucky Fried Chicken when he was 62. Walt Disney, at 52 years old, after several failures, had his dream for Disneyland come true. Nelson Mandela received the Nobel Peace Prize when he was 75 years old.

Ask participants to individually write down some examples of people they know or have heard of who demonstrate that we can keep learning and producing as long as we keep our mind and bodies active.

Discussion Questions

1. Do you personally know people (parents, friends, colleagues, and others) who clearly show the "old dog" adage to be wrong?

2. Why do you believe these people keep creating and learning even at advanced ages? What characteristics or attitudes do they possess?

3. Do any of you work with people older than you? Do you feel you appreciate and value their potential?

IQ vs. EQ

OBJECTIVE

- To show that in today's workplace emotional intelligence is just as important as cognitive intelligence

Materials

None

Time

15 to 20 minutes

Procedure

We all recognize that a person's knowledge and skills are imperative for success in today's society. However, it is becoming increasingly acknowledged that one's EQ, *Emotional Quotient*, is equally, if not even more, important. Ask group members to think of a person—coworker, manager, relative, or someone else—who clearly manifests great job skills and knowledge but may well lack the "people skills" so needed today.

Discussion Questions

1. How many of you personally know people who are clearly intellectual "tens" but emotional "zeroes"?
2. Have any of you had previous supervisors who fit this picture?
3. What are some tips or techniques you've found helpful in these cases?
4. How would one go about telling a manager of his or her challenge in this area?

Right Brain, Left Brain?

Materials

Copies of Right-Brain, Left-Brain
Lateralization Chart (provided)

Time

15 to 20 minutes

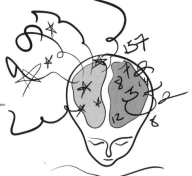

Procedure

As mentioned earlier in the chapter, we are whole-brained creatures; we are not right-brained or left-brained! *Both hemispheres work together* to process and store information. Each hemisphere, however, does specialize in certain functions, and individuals do tend to have hemispheric preferences. These preferences influence not only our learning styles but also our personalities and ultimately our behaviors. Neither hemispheric preference is superior to the other; some individuals actually have no preference. Distribute copies of the Right-Brain, Left-Brain Lateralization Chart. Request that participants discuss the following questions in triads.

Discussion Questions

1. As you reviewed the right-brain, left-brain specialties, did you think/feel that you tended to have one hemispheric preference over the other?
2. How do you think/feel this preference shows up in your personality?
3. Is it very obvious to you when a colleague has a hemisphere preference different from yours?
4. In working relationships, what have you learned that will help increase better understanding of others?

Right-Brain, Left-Brain Lateralization Chart

Left-Brain Specialization	Right-Brain Specialization
Sequencing (lists)	Spatial (maps, puzzles)
Logic	Imagination
Time	Artistic awareness
Analysis	Depth perception
Number skills	Musical activities
Reasoning	Face recognition
Speech	Dreaming
Reading	3-D forms
Writing	Emotional perception
Counting and math	Sense of humor
Symbol recognition	Insight
Processing external stimuli	Processing internal messages

What If?

OBJECTIVE
- To demonstrate the brain's power to come up with innovative and imaginative responses to unusual questions

Materials

Nerf (foam) balls or other objects that can be tossed safely from person to person, paper, pens

Time

10 to 15 minutes

Procedure

This activity calls for imagination and out-of-the-box thinking. Encourage innovative, outlandish, or even silly questions. For example, "What if we all lived to be two hundred years old?" or "What if the average workweek was twenty hours?"

Give everyone a moment or two to write down some "What if?" questions. Remember, they can pertain to a real-world event or be completely hypothetical.

Request that the group form small circles (five to eight participants each) and ask for a volunteer at each circle to begin the exercise. Give each of the volunteers a ball (or other object to be thrown); ask that they pose their first question and then quickly toss the ball to another participant in their circle. The participant who catches the ball must quickly answer the question, promptly ask his or her own question, and quickly toss the ball to yet another participant in the circle. Continue for three or four questions or as long as time permits.

Discussion Questions

1. How could this activity be used at your office?

2. Did you discover some unusual solutions to the questions?

3. Could this activity be applied to real-life scenarios?

4. Have you ever heard of other "What if?" questions that might have developed into some commonly used household products or other ingenious inventions?

The Dead Moose Society

OBJECTIVE

- To openly and safely express attitudes and opinions about sensitive or awkward conditions in the work environment

Materials

Copies of The Dead Moose Society handout (provided)

Time

15 to 30 minutes

Procedure

Explain that in many companies and organizations there are issues, challenges, and problems that everyone is aware of, but they simply don't think it's "safe" or politically correct to speak openly about them. This activity allows participants to openly and candidly discuss these situations with the understanding that what happens in the training session stays in the training session.

Form teams of three or four participants. Invite the participants to be as open and honest in their discussion as their comfort level allows. Caution them that the purpose of this game is not to accuse or point fingers; rather, it's an opportunity to discuss a problem or impending challenge to explore potential resolutions. Provide participants with a copy of The Dead Moose Society handout and request that they discuss with their teammates questions 1–6, found at the end of the handout.

Tip

Use this activity only after the group members have established a high level of trust with one another.

Discussions Question

1. Ask for responses from the groups for all six questions on the handout.

The Dead Moose Society

This is the story of the dead moose. As the fable goes, most, if not all, organizations and associations have experienced the overt—or, more often, covert—sightings of this troublesome creature. A metaphor for something that's obviously wrong or counterproductive within the organization, a "dead moose" can be offensive, oppressive, fearsome, or even threatening—and yet everyone is hesitant to openly discuss the big, smelly thing.

This dead moose may lurk under the table of corporate cultures or sometimes right on top of it. It may poison the atmosphere of meetings and block the progress of teams. Its presence can be loathsome, repugnant, even hateful—and always counterproductive. So if it's so apparent that the burdensome dead moose is in attendance, why doesn't someone simply shout, "We have a dead moose here; I don't believe that we should have to stumble around it every day, pretending that it's not here. Do we all think it will just go away if we ignore it?"

Let's start by acknowledging that there just might be a dead moose in this very room. Maybe you can't see it, but I bet you can sense its presence. Maybe you've seen one in your own office—or maybe it's been there so long that you're not even conscious of it anymore.

Let's look at a few questions to see if indeed there is a dead moose or two at your workplace, and if not (lucky you!), how to deal with one appropriately if it does show up. *It's important to be as open and honest as possible during this discussion.*

1. What would a dead moose look like? How would it appear in one's company?

2. Have you ever seen one in your company or office—maybe even in your own cubicle?

3. What are some harmful effects or results of having this creature in your company?

4. If it's really there, why do we continue to let it haunt us? Fear of being called a whistle-blower? Fear of reprisal from colleagues?

5. What are two or three cases where you've seen this moose?

6. What are two or three things you and/or your colleagues can do to alleviate these situations or bring things out that need to be discussed openly and candidly?

4

May I Have Your Attention! Make the Move from Attention to Memory

I sometimes worry about my short attention span, but not for long.

—Herb Caen

Chapter Highlights

This chapter presents models/theories on attention, with an opportunity to practice your selective and focused attention. Also included are strategies for increasing your attention abilities. Hint: the ball's in your court!

"*Attention*," according to the *Medical Dictionary Online*, is "focusing on certain aspects of current experience to the exclusion of others. It is the act of heeding or taking notice or concentrating." Attention is considered the most important component of forming new memory, but it is also highly influenced by past memory.

In the last 50 years, input (stimuli) to the brain has increased more than ten thousand times per second. For example, if you are 50 years old, your brain is receiving ten thousand times more information than it did when you were born.

Not only are we bombarded with additional information, but we're also—due to modern technology—inundated with interruptions (which create the necessity to refocus) from phone calls, e-mails, text messages, and tweets.

Dr. Torkel Klingberg of the Stockholm Brain Institute, author of *The Overflowing Brain: Information Overload and the Limits of Working Memory*, states in his online article "Research and Tools to Thrive in the Cognitive Age," written for SharpBrain (sharpbrain.com), "a survey of workplaces in the United States found that the personnel were interrupted and distracted roughly every three minutes and that people working on a computer had on average eight windows open at the same time." He goes on to pose four critical questions concerning these cognitive demands flooding our brains: "How do we deal with the daily influx of information that our inundated mental capacities are faced with? At what point does our stone-age brain become insufficient? Will we be able to train our brains effectively to increase brain capacity in order to stay in-step with our inexorable lifestyles? Or will we be stricken with attention deficits because of brain overload?" Theories abound, and researchers persist in their quest to better understand how we process incoming stimuli and subsequently form memory—and how future brains will cope with the rising cognitive demands.

Models and Theories of Attention

According to Dr. Lawrence M. Ward, University of British Columbia, there are usually at least three aspects of attention: *orienting*, *filtering*, and *searching*. *Orienting*, Dr. Ward states, is the ability to adjust our sensory receptors toward one set of stimuli and away from others, thus selecting some stimuli and thereby excluding other stimuli. *Filtering* is the pulling out of certain information from the already selected stimuli. *Searching* occurs when we are aware of what stimuli we wish to focus on but unaware of where to find it and therefore have to look for it.

Psychologist Dr. Michael Posner, an eminent researcher and professor of neuroscience in the field of attention at the University of Oregon, formed his hypothesis and developed a model on how the brain processes visual information. His model was based on the brain's utilizing three separate systems to attend to stimuli: the *Arousal Network*, the *Orienting Network*, and the *Executive Network*. To explain these terms, let's look at the following story.

Picture this: You stop by the supermarket on your way home from the office. As you're making your way down the frozen-food aisle, you realize there are no products you need, so you decide to make your way to the next aisle. According to Dr. Posner, your *Arousal Network* is at work here. It is a general level of attention wherein you observe your surroundings yet remain alert to anything that might be out of the ordinary.

Just then, a little girl about four or five years old comes charging around the corner, screaming, "Help, help, he's going to get me!" A split second later a huge man bursts into sight, chasing her. Suddenly, you transition into your *Orienting Network*. No longer just strolling down the aisle, casually taking in nonspecific stimuli, you shift and become very specific about where your attention is directed. Is the little girl OK? Does she know this man?

Before your thought is fully formed, the man scoops the little girl up in his arms and tenderly yet firmly says, "Daddy said no running, sweetheart." The little girl giggles and replies, "I didn't mean to run, Daddy—I think my feet just started to move too fast." You've now moved to your *Executive Network*. This is the *"What do I make of this information?"* stage. Your questions concerning the little girl's safety have been satisfied, and you continue your shopping.

The basis of the clinical model presented by Drs. McKay Moore Sohlberg of the University of Oregon and Catherine Mateer of the University of Victoria focused on the attention recovery process of patients who experienced brain damage after being in a coma. Each of the following five types of attention (focus, sustained attention, selective attention, alternating attention, and divided attention) was considered increasingly difficult as their patients recovered from their injuries.

- **Focused attention:** Focusing on certain aspects or stimuli (visual, auditory, tactile, gustatory) of a current experience to the exclusion of others. Basically this is what we mean when we use the word *attention* in general.
- **Sustained attention:** When focused attention becomes extended, one is able to maintain a consistent behavioral response during continuous and repetitive activity. This type of attention now involves both short-term memory and some motivation. One might also refer to this type of attention as *concentration* or *attention span*. An example of an activity requiring sustained attention would be to count backward from a hundred by threes.
- **Selective attention:** This level of attention refers to the ability to maintain behavioral or cognitive performance in the presence of distracting or competing stimuli. Therefore it incorporates the concept of ignoring one set of characteristics or data to decipher another set (also known as *freedom from distractibility*).
- **Alternating attention:** The capability for mental flexibility. This type of attention allows individuals to shift their focus of attention between tasks that require different cognitive characteristics. A model called *divided attention* was once believed to allow individuals to respond to tasks simultaneously (multitasking). Scientific brain imaging now shows that there is no such thing as multitasking. Our brains simply allow us, in a matter of miniseconds, to move rapidly from one mental task to another as the brain shifts from activating different areas.
- **Divided attention:** This level of attention refers to the ability to respond simultaneously to multiple tasks or multiple task demands. It may involve alternating attention in a rapid manner from one stimulus to another. (We now know that the brain processes information

in a sequential manner, unable to pay attention to two different stimuli at the same time. It is, however, important that the brain function with flexibility, enabling it to sequence at a faster rate.)

Improving and Enhancing Attention

Our brains are constantly and consistently being bombarded with new data, information, and energy via all kinds of sensory input (visual, olfactory, auditory, kinesthetic, gustatory, and even intuitive). Every second, millions of bits of information inundate our senses and compete for our awareness. How does the brain decide which information to pay attention to? Research indicates that what's *important* to your particular brain is determined by past experiences, interests, fears, and desires—all found in your preexisting networks. We use previous experiences, interests, and perceptions to predict *where* and *for how long* we should place our focus.

The bottom line is that we don't pay attention to the uninteresting, boring, or nonthreatening things. The information that seizes your attention is related to information that (a) already exists in your memory; (b) is connected to your interest, which means you have in some way placed a value on it (good or bad, high or low); and (c) is in the scope of your awareness.

It's a matter of choice—an attitude you must take if you truly *want* to focus and remember more and better. Your level of motivation to be alert, stay focused, and concentrate is squarely in your hands—or, rather, your mind!

So why don't we just pay better attention? Research indicates that when we stray from our intended target of attention, it may be due to a brain disconnect. A study conducted by Dr. Daniel Weissman of the University of Michigan indicated that when attention wavers, the communication between regions of the brain relating to self-control, vision, and language decreases. According to Dr. Weissman, this is the equivalent of a disconnect.

Some medical studies have shown that intense involvement in TV and video games may contribute to some attention disorders by overwhelming the brain. Cleverly, some brain-training software companies have taken the technology produced by this TV/video craze and channeled it to better use. One such company, Unique Logic + Technology, has created a computerized video game, Play Attention, which claims to teach and/or retrain the brain to increase attention and concentration—it's both challenging and entertaining. Numerous other companies are also jumping on board this multimillion-dollar industry.

If you're not quite ready for brain-training software, the following chart lists some strategies that will provide you with more opportunities to hone your attention skills—without any bells or whistles!

Strategies for Increasing Your Attention Abilities
- Stare at the flame of a candle.
- Find a spot on the wall and stare at it.
- Sit quietly and focus on your breath coming in and going out.
- Count backward from a hundred.
- Count backward from a hundred by threes.
- Watch the second hand on a clock.
- Pay attention to the sensations in one part of the body.
- Attend to a particular sight, sound, taste, or smell.
- Attend to your thoughts or emotions.

Brain Teaser #3

OBJECTIVES
- To practice creativity or creative problem solving
- To fill time
- To do something "just for fun"

Materials

Copies of the Brain Teaser #3 handout (provided)

Time

5 to 15 minutes

Procedure

Give each audience member a copy of the handout. Explain that each of the 16 frames or boxes in the quiz suggests a well-known slogan, phrase, or saying and that the task is to decipher the hidden message in each box. To get the exercise started and ensure that the group has a clear understanding of how the quiz works, provide an answer to any one of the frames. Allow participants two to three minutes to do the quiz individually. Then suggest that they pair up with a partner and see how many more frames they can solve together. Allow another two to three minutes. Then, starting with frame #1, begin soliciting answers from the group for each of the frames. If a response is fairly close to the "right" answer, simply paraphrase the answer to make it the correct one.

Discussion Questions

1. How many frames were you able to solve correctly on your own?
2. How many more did you solve when you worked with others?
3. When working with partners, did you come up with alternate answers?
4. Are you able to create some of these brain teasers yourself? Try one now. Is it easier solving a brain teaser or creating a brain teaser?

Brain Teaser #3

Decipher the hidden meaning of each box. Each of these describes a well-known saying or slogan.

1. BR AIN	**2.** Corres4pondent	**3.** VERS.	**4.** CC TICKETS
5. NOS⅂IW	**6.** wonder	**7.** HR HR WORKING	**8.** GO IT IT IT IT!
9. WORLD WORLD WORLD	**10.** CC FIRE	**11.** ENG LI SH	**12.** YO MIND UR·
13. C H THE THE E THE THE A THE THE P THE THE E THE THE R THE THE	**14.** M.D. M.D.	**15.** 'TIM	**16.** PLAYPAUSE

Brain Teaser #3 Answers

1. split brain

2. foreign correspondent

3. abbreviated version

4. season tickets

5. Flip Wilson

6. small wonder

7. working after hours

8. go for it

9. worlds apart

10. cease fire

11. broken English

12. you are out of your mind

13. cheaper by the dozen

14. paramedics or paradox

15. the beginning of time

16. round of applause

Just Leave Me Alone

Materials

None

Time

10 to 15 minutes

Procedure

As most of us know, working at home is very common in today's workforce. In fact, many companies have their entire sales force working virtually. While there are those who suggest that the virtual office is merely an excuse to escape the workplace and spend more time on non-job-related tasks—and subsequently not get the job done—studies have suggested that this is not the case at all. Explain to the group that they will be working in teams of three to four people and will be discussing the following questions.

Discussion Questions

1. How many of you are currently working in a virtual situation?
2. What has been the perception of your office colleagues?
3. Are you finding that you are indeed more productive?
4. For those of you who are "virtual," what are some of the tips you've learned that you can share with others?
5. For those of you who'd like to sell your manager on your going virtual, what are some of the arguments he or she may counter with?
6. For those of you working at your cube or in an office, what are some of the interruptions or distractions you face?
7. Any hints as to how these can be handled?

The Alphabet Game

OBJECTIVES
- To give attendees a potpourri of fun and easy ways to get involved
- To show how easily some memories can be retrieved

Materials

Copies of The Alphabet Game List (provided), a stopwatch that can time two minutes

Time

15 to 20 minutes

Procedure

Distribute copies of The Alphabet Activity List or display it on a PowerPoint slide.

Form teams of three or four attendees and ask participants to choose one item from the activity list (more items may be chosen if time permits) and build a two-minute story based on a memory related to the selected topic. Give the group about one minute to think silently about how they're going to report their story to their team members—in only two minutes. Identify each team's first storyteller and begin the stopwatch. Announce every two minutes that the next person is now to begin telling his or her story—until all four in each team have shared their stories.

Discussion Questions

1. As you perused the list, did some words jump out at you as conjuring memories from the past?
2. Did you have difficulty relating to any of the topics? Was it easy or difficult to retrieve aspects of those memories?
3. Did you find you wanted more time to share your story (or perhaps to just relive it yourself)?
4. Did you find that you wanted to hear more about another teammate's story than the two-minute time period permitted?

The Alphabet Game List

A. Adventure

B. Birthday party

C. College

D. Drive-in

E. Educator

F. First date

G. Grandparents

H. High School Prom

I. Interviews

J. Jargon

K. Kindergarten

L. Laughter

M. Minister

N. Next-Door Neighbors

O. Oval Office

P. Peter Principle

Q. Quandary

R. Recess

S. Spring

T. Trip

U. Umbrella

V. Visionary

W. Weather

X. X-Rays

Y. Yardstick

Z. Zoos

The Official Stand-Up Person

OBJECTIVES
- To prove how essential it is to intersperse learning with breaks and fun activities
- To prevent the dreaded audience drift

Materials

None

Time

1 to 2 minutes

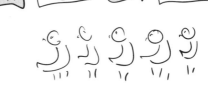

Procedure

Advise the group you need help with a fun activity. As we discussed earlier in the chapter, the average span of attention for most adults is not half a day, 90 minutes, or even 45 minutes; rather, it's as brief as three or four minutes. Explain that while they'll have a midmorning and midafternoon break, and you'll do your best to keep things rolling, you know that their attention is likely to wander.

With that in mind, jokingly ask the group, "Who here has a really short attention span?" In most cases, the group will point to one person. This usually gets a laugh. You can then ask this "volunteer" for help. (If no one volunteers, pick out a smiling face in the front of the room.)

This person's job for the morning (or for the day) will be to serve as the audience's "Official Stand-Up Person." Tell the volunteer that your job, as the facilitator, is an easy one since you'll be moving around quite a bit. However, as a captive audience, the job of your participants is more difficult.

So, anytime during the course of the morning (or afternoon) that your "Stand-Up Person" feels it's time for a quick break, all he or she needs to do is to stand up, and you in turn, will "shut up"—and we'll all take a quick break.

Tip

This is for use with programs of a half day or longer.

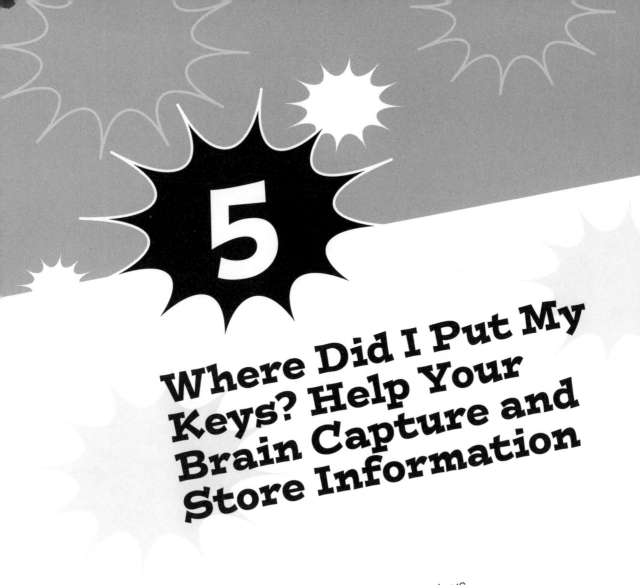

5

Where Did I Put My Keys? Help Your Brain Capture and Store Information

Memory is the diary that we all carry about with us.

—Oscar Wilde

Chapter Highlights

This chapter introduces the reader to the process of forming and storing memory. It provides strategies for keeping your memory sharp and tips for the leader/trainer/educator to promote memory retention in the learner.

So you say you are gifted with a flawless memory? You think you can recall with absolute certainty every single detail of a memorable event? Not so, say the renowned scientists who pursue the mysteries of the human memory and the various—many, as yet, unknown—processes involved. It seems that every time you recall an existing memory you merge new information with your past memories, thus allowing for memory contamination—*each* and *every* time you relive that experience.

The Memory Process

A common definition of *memory* is an activity utilizing mental capabilities to recall, recover, and reproduce information that has been retained or preserved based on previous learnings and experiences. However, the larger memory *process* involves much more than just the skill of recalling or retrieving information. The actual *memory process* also includes the acquisition and consolidation of the trillions of bits of information presented to you throughout your days and nights. This highly complex process entails communication between multiple areas of the brain—the hippocampus, amygdala, thalamus, hypothalamus, and cerebral cortex—together with countless hormones, neurons, and neurotransmitters. To date, researchers are still confounded by the mysteries of memory, and controversial hypotheses abound.

Research, both recent and long passed, has provided us with an abundance of theories and models—all formulated in an effort to explain and clarify this complicated processing system. The following model is one of the most widely accepted understandings of the memory process. It demonstrates (in a very, very simplified format) how *formation, encoding, retention,* and *retrieval* interrelate.

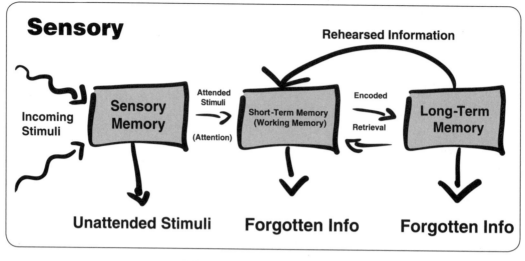

FIGURE 5.1 Memory process

- **Incoming stimuli:** Our brains are constantly being bombarded with new data, information, and energy via sensory input. Sensory memory, which disintegrates rapidly, acts as a screen, sifting through the incoming stimuli and selecting (by means of attention) only stimuli that appear important or valuable at that point in time. These *keeper stimuli* are then passed on to short-term memory. (See Figure 5.1.)
- **Short-term memory:** This memory is also termed *working memory* because it functions as a temporary holding area or scratch pad for recall of recently acquired information. One can hold a limited amount of information (approximately seven bits, plus or minus two) in short-term memory for from a few seconds to one to three minutes. Rehearsal or review and "chunking" (discussed in the tips later in the chapter) can help increase this time frame. On the other hand, interference (the exposure to further information) can decrease the retention rate—hence the urgency to dial that phone number as soon as possible after you've looked it up. If you pay close enough attention—stay focused and concentrate—thanks to the communication between your amygdala and hippocampus, and the subsequent release of cortisol or epinephrine, this new information will become encoded and then stored in your long-term memory.

- **Long-term memory:** This is the storage area especially designed to hold memory for up to a lifetime. Memories are usually preserved because they (1) hold some significant meaning (your significant other's birthday or your son's allergy to peanuts); (2) allow for easier life functioning (road signs, company policies, cultural practices); or (3) have made an emotional impact (first date, favorite love song, or an attack—physical or emotional).

Types of Long-Term Memory

There are two types of memory: *declarative* (explicit) and *nondeclarative or procedural* (implicit). (See Figure 5.2.) Declarative memory is broken down further into two categories: episodic memory and semantic memory. *Episodic memory* holds the history of the experiences and events of our

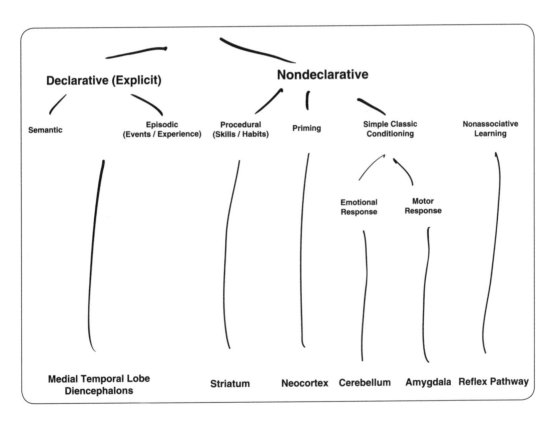

FIGURE 5.2 Taxonomy of long-term memory

life. Because episodic memory stores memory in serial form, we can recall and reconstruct past events or experiences, identifying at what point in our life they took place. **Semantic memory** is concerned with facts, records, and concepts—things like the multiplication tables, word meanings, and color recognition, which need not be chronological.

Memory Retrieval

We've discussed only in very basic terms the complex process of memory. However, when asked to describe what *memory* is, most folks will automatically think only of the retrieval aspect of the process. This is probably because retrieval is the feature of the process that most of us use to gauge how well our memory is working—or not working! *Recall, recollection*, and *recognition* are all key forms of memory retrieval that allow access to information stored in your memory banks.

- **Recall:** This is when information is reproduced from a memory without need for any cues (hints, prompts, or clues) from any part of the existing memory. An example of using this type of memory is when you perform a fill-in-the-blank exam.
- **Recognition:** In this case additional information serves as a retrieval cue, prompting one to acknowledge that this is not the first exposure to the information. An example of using this type of memory is when completing a multiple-choice exam.
- **Recollection:** Not unlike recognition, this form of memory retrieval requires cues. But the cues are obtained from incomplete, limited, or partial memories, which then serve as hints for reorganizing or reconstructing the information for use in the present situation. An example of using this type of memory is when completing an essay exam.

According to John Medina, in his book *Brain Rules*, the learning or encoding process that occurs, enabling new information to become stored in your long-term memory, is still a vast unsolved mystery. He states, however, that based on what we do know, the process is similar to running a blender without the lid on. He states that when the encoding/learning process occurs, "the information is literally sliced into discrete pieces as it enters the brain and splattered all over the insides of our mind. . . . The information is fragmented and redistributed the instant the information is encountered." And if it's stored in multiple areas, it must be retrieved from multiple areas.

So when you're looking at an image, your brain will address each bit of stimulus or information separately, identifying it and then sending it to its appropriate sensory source location. Hence diagonal lines and vertical lines are stored in separate areas of the brain, as are different colors and even vowels and consonants. Words themselves contain three different types of information: semantic (meaning), phonological (sound), and lexical (letters). Each of these is located in separate parts of the brain. Based on this storage arrangement, it's obvious that when it comes time to retrieve a memory, the brain has much work to do. It has to access all the information from these various areas of the brain, reassembling and reuniting thousands of bits of information into something resembling the original information presented.

So think again about that perfect day, of which you remember *every* detail. Are you still certain?

Tip of the Tongue

We've all had the experience—that word you can't seem to get out. It's there, on the "tip of your tongue," as they say. You know it; you know what it means; you know how many syllables it has; you might even know what it rhymes with or its initial letter. The word seems to be cloaked in fog, drifting teasingly just out of reach. Then, at some point when you least expect it, it just magically appears. Why? A study by Drs. Lori E. James and Deborah M. Burke, published in the *Journal of Experimental Psychology: Learning, Memory, and Cognition*, suggests that there is a weak neural net connection between the meaning of the word (held in semantic memory in one region of the brain) and the sound of the word (held in phonologic memory in another part of the brain.) Since connections grow stronger when used and weaker when not used, they hypothesized that when the tip-of-the-tongue word finally does materialize, it may be because you've just experienced a word with a similar sound. Should you worry about these episodes? Apparently not! Yes, tip-of-the-tongue experiences do tend to occur more often as we age, and it takes longer for the misplaced word to reappear. However, scientists suspect this happens because as we age we tend to fall into patterns, doing the same activities over and over. What's recommended, not surprisingly, is to keep reading, do more crossword puzzles, learn new words, and keep those connections active.

Use It or Lose It!

Memory is like muscle strength; if you don't use it, you lose it. It becomes flabby and lazy and simply doesn't work as rapidly or as effectively.

Following are some strategies for keeping your brain strong and your mental functions sharp:

- **Pay attention:** Explore the various methods of paying attention—and remember what we discussed in Chapter 4; it's your choice.
- **Review-reflect-rehearse:** Try this immediately after gaining new information, at timed intervals, and just before sleep. Use flash cards when appropriate.
- **Sleep:** Getting the proper amount of sleep increases energy, attention, and concentration. It also decreases stress and plays a crucial role in memory consolidation.
- **Exercise:** Aerobic exercise increases the level of glucose (brain food) and oxygen to the brain.
- **Nutrition:** Eating a healthy diet—one consisting of fruits, vegetables, whole grains and good fats—will nurture and stimulate brain function and sharpen the memory.
- **No multitasking:** It's a myth! It's really *multiswitching*. Focus on just one thing at a time (that also means no music, unless it's the sounds of nature).
- **Relax:** Take deep breaths, meditate, or do yoga.
- **Organize:** Write it on the calendar, use Post-It notes, or create a filing system.

- **Write things down:** And then rewrite them again! Take notes, make a flowchart, do a mind map, draw figures, or use colored pencils.
- **Laugh:** Don't worry; be happy! Laughter suppresses cortisol (stress chemical) levels, lowers blood pressure, and decreases arrhythmia.
- **Minimize stress:** Stress increases the production of cortisol, which inhibits the learning process. Go easy on yourself.
- **Preread:** Read or review your course syllabus, outline, agenda, and/or relevant material prior to attending your workshop, meeting, or training.
- **Minimize/eliminate smoking:** Smoking restricts blood flow to the brain.
- **Consciously decide to remember:** Commitment goes a long way!
- **Use mnemonic devices:** See the examples that follow in "Tips for Promoting Memory Retention."
- **And if you're really curious, try neurofeedback:** Scientists say that this technology, based on biofeedback, could help people improve memory. It's a noninvasive, drug-free, and relaxing way of balancing and harmonizing brain frequencies.

Tips for Promoting Memory Retention

- **Incorporate as many learning styles as possible:** Use a variety of visual, auditory, and kinesthetic modalities.
- **Let your audience know what to expect:** Prepare audience members by providing an agenda or overview at the beginning of each heading, topic, or section. The brain will be more prepared to receive the stimuli.
- **Keep stress levels low:** High stress levels impair memory accuracy and thus compromise the opportunity for a positive learning experience.
- **Engage emotions:** Weave emotional triggers into your learning environment. It is clear that we remember emotionally charged experiences more easily than those that are dull or uninteresting. Positive emotions are remembered better than negative emotions, and, not surprisingly, the stronger the emotions aroused, the stronger the impact on memory.

- **New information introduction:** Gradually introduce new information and be certain to establish the basics before presenting the complex. Tie in the new information with existing information. Then review and repeat new information at timed intervals.
- **Provide frequent on-your-feet breaks:** Movement actually reenergizes the body *and* the brain. According to David A. Sousa, in his book *How the Brain Learns*, "When we sit for more than 20 minutes, our blood pools in our seat and our feet. By getting up and moving, we recirculate that blood. Within a minute, there is about 15 percent more blood in our brain. We do think better on our feet!"
- **Incorporate novelty:** Do something drastically different from what you've been doing or saying—*every 10 minutes*. The brain needs a respite, a break, a change in venue—just about *every 10 minutes*! The brain loves novelty. When something novel is presented to the brain, the sensory receptors become aroused (they're interested; they're excited). However, if this stimulus continues repeatedly without variation, the once-aroused receptors shut down or terminate their state of arousal (they're bored; it's time to ignore). Vary the quality or quantity of the stimuli and—voilà—the sensory receptors snap to attention and spring into action. It's no small surprise that your sensory receptors shut down their aroused state when forced to listen to someone speaking in a monotone.
- **Encourage doodling:** Doodles, even if they seem irrelevant to the topic at hand, are valuable to the recall process, especially regarding details.
- **Include mnemonics:** (Drop the *m*; it's pronounced "ne-MON-ics.") These are techniques and systems used to support and enhance the memory process by incorporating rhymes, rules, phrases, acronyms, and other such devices. It is based on the Greek word *mneme* ("memory"), with historical records indicating its utilization as early as 477 B.C. For example:
  - **Peg method:** A technique to remember a series of numbers such as phone numbers, account numbers, or password numbers. To use this technique, begin by mentally assigning a word, figure, or icon to each number from 0 to 9. Each image may be a word that

rhymes with the number, resembles the shape of the number, or in some way represents the number to you. An example would be to create in your mind the image of a pencil to represent the number 1 (looks like a 1), an image of a swan to represent the number 2 (the neck of a swan looks like the number 2), a tree to represent number 3 (*tree* rhymes with *three*), and a fork to represent the number 4 (there are usually four prongs on a fork). Then connect the created images together in a colorful or dramatic story.

- **Method of loci (Roman-room method):** Used by ancient orators, this is a technique for remembering significant amounts of information, be it a speech or a list of items. To use this technique, you first think of a familiar route and specific points or objects along the way (your commute to work, a walk from one end of your home to the other, your morning or evening walk, and the like). You then mentally place visual images representing the items on your list or the key points in your speech at landmarks along your route. The number of landmarks you decide on will be determined by the number of items/points you wish to remember. Then simply mentally retrace the route to recall the information. This is the origin of the expression "in the first place."

- **Chunking:** Based on the "seven plus or minus two" theory for holding information in our short-term, working memory, chunking is a system of grouping numbers and information into smaller chunks for easier retrieval. For example, to remember the number 03181972 is more difficult than remembering 03 18 1972 (date). This is because it's easier to hold groups of these 2s, 3s, or 4s rather than a long string of digits.

- **Rhymes, rhythm, and repetition:** A fun method of remembering used since childhood. Remember learning the alphabet or "30 days hath September, April, June, and November?" Useful for rote memory, but not for understanding information.

- **Nonsense sentences:** In this technique, the first letter of each word in a nonsense sentence represents or is a part of the word you wish to remember. If you've ever taken music lessons, you likely memorized the treble clef with the sentence "Every good boy does fine."

Medical students sometimes use this technique to memorize parts of the body's anatomy. For instance, "The brain's **c**erebrum consists of the **p**arietals, **o**ccipitals, **t**emporals, and **f**rontal" can be turned into "Crazy pigs often take flight." Again, this method does not provide an understanding of the information; it is used only for rote memory.

Are You Smarter than a Ten-Year-Old?

Material

None

Time

10 to 15 minutes

Procedure

Ask how many are familiar with the popular TV show "Are You Smarter than a Fifth Grader?" Acknowledge that while some fifth-graders may indeed seem more "book smart" than adults, adults memorized many of the same facts and figures "way back when." As time progressed, we replaced those rote memories because we needed to use our brains for more current and important information.

Discussion Questions

1. How many of you have seen this TV show? How many have "flunked" the questions?
2. Doubtless, most of us knew these answers when we were kids. Why can't we remember these facts now? How important is it to you to remember these facts now?
3. How have your methods of learning new material changed as opposed to "way back when"?

I Can Dream, Can't I?

OBJECTIVES

- To illustrate that the brain is always working
- To show that our dreams tend to replay thoughts or actions we experienced during the day

Materials

None

Time

10 to 15 minutes

Procedure

Ask the group to form teams of two or three and ask them if they can remember having had any dreams last night. (Note: we all dream, but most of us forget our dreams by the time we wake up.) Ask them to describe a dream they had and then ask them to reconstruct this dream as memory allows. While dreams may appear to have seamless continuity, it may well be that these dreams are really a collage or a collection of happenings we have experienced during the day. If they can recognize the "bits and pieces" of their dreams as a reflection of thoughts or activities they had yesterday, they may be able to better appreciate that the brain is always working.

Discussion Questions

1. How many of you had a dream last night?
2. As you recall your dream now, do you remember if some elements in the dream were actually experienced yesterday?
3. As you discussed your dream with your partner, did any part of your dream seem totally outlandish or ridiculous?
4. Did any of you wake up during the evening with an answer to a problem you may have been thinking about before you went to sleep?

Hi, There—Next! Part 1

Materials

None

Time

5 to 10 minutes

Procedure

Explain to the group that in just a minute or two they'll be asked to get up and go around the room and meet three or four new friends. Instruct them that they will have only two or three minutes to do so. After they have spent the two to three minutes meeting new people, ask them to take their seats.

Discussion Questions

1. How many of you met at least three or four new friends?
2. How many of you can right now tell me the names of the three or four new people you just met? Why or why not?
3. How often do you meet someone and within seconds forget the person's name? Do you find it easier to remember faces?

Hi, There—Next! Part 2

OBJECTIVE
- To demonstrate that honing our focusing skills and using a memory technique promotes retention of names

Materials

None

Time

5 to 10 minutes

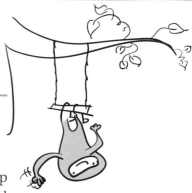

Procedure

Use this activity as a follow-up to "Hi, There—Next! Part 1." Thank the group for their participation in "Round 1" and explain that you are now going to provide an opportunity for them to (1) learn a memory technique and (2) immediately put that new technique to use by again meeting three to four different people in a two- to three-minute period of time. And you're going to show them that they can have fun doing this.

Here is the technique:

1. Listen! Make sure you hear the name correctly. If necessary, request that the person spell his or her name.
2. Repeat the name two or three times in the ensuing conversation.
3. If time permits, try using an association or image that would correspond with the name. For example, with the name A. J. Albrecht, you might imagine this person owns a pet bird—a blue jay (A.J.) that perches on a wall that is constructed completely (all) of bricks (Albrecht). With the name Haley Quin, you might visualize the person running into the Q Inn (Quinn) while the storm overhead showers large hail (Haley) stones.

Go to it! Invite group members to meet three to four new people and after two to three minutes ask them to be seated.

Discussion Questions

1. How many of you met at least three or four new friends?

2. How many names do you remember this time?

3. Did you remember more names this time than in the previous activity? Why or why not?

Thanks for the Memories

OBJECTIVE

• To demonstrate that some information from our past has been stored in our long-term memory banks and can be recalled

Materials

Copies of the Thanks for the Memories handout (provided)

Time

5 to 10 minutes

Procedure

Give each participant a copy of the Thanks for the Memories handout. Ask them to put their "memory caps" on to retrieve the answers to questions or complete the slogans from past commercials, TV shows, etc. Make the point that information stored in our memory banks can be recalled even if it has not been accessed for a long time. To demonstrate how the game is played, give participants one of the answers. If the group includes several Gen Y–ers, ask them to pair up with another, older member (these slogans may not be in their memory banks). Give participants two to three minutes to work on the quiz individually and then ask them to pair up with a partner in an attempt to solve additional slogans. Allow two or three more minutes.

Discussion Questions

1. How many of these questions were you able to answer correctly on your own?

2. Do these questions bring back some memories?

3. When might you guess was the last time you even heard—or thought—about these items?

4. Were you surprised as to how quickly some of these answers jumped right out at you?

Thanks for the Memories

Here are some well-known slogans, commercials, and TV stars from the past. See how your memory serves you! Jot down your answers in the space provided.

1. "You're in good hands with _____."

2. "Where's the _____?"

3. "Liar, liar, _____ _____ _____!"

4. Muhammad Ali's former name was _____ _____.

5. "Lions and tigers and bears, _____ _____!"

6. "Breakfast of champions: _____."

7. "I found my thrill _____ _____ _____."

8. Name the Beatles: _____, _____, _____,
_____

9. Pogo met the enemy and " _____ _____
_____!"

10. Sonny and _____

11. "_____ _____ builds strong bodies 12 ways."

12. "You'll wonder where the yellow went _____ _____
_____ _____ _____ _____
_____."

13. "Hey kids, what time is it?" "_____ _____

_____ _____!"

14. "_____—a little dab'll do ya!"

15. "_____ _____—when you care enough to send the very best."

16. In "Frasier," Marty's dog is named _____.

17. "What's in your wallet?" _____ _____

18. "M-I-C-_____ – _____ – _____

_____ – _____ – _____ – _____ –

_____"

19. "It's the real thing—_____."

20. "Good to the last drop: _____ _____

_____."

21. "Let _____ put you in the driver's seat."

22. "Just the facts, Ma'am," said _____ _____.

23. "See the USA in your _____."

24. _____—57 varieties

25. "Fly the friendly skies."—_____ _____

Thanks for the Memories Answers

1. "You're in Good Hands with **Allstate**."

2. "Where's the **Beef**?" (Wendy's)

3. "Liar, liar, **pants on fire**!"

4. Muhammad Ali's former name was **Cassius Clay**.

5. "Lions and tigers and bears, **oh my**!"

6. Breakfast of Champions: **Wheaties**

7. "I found my thrill **on Blueberry Hill**."

8. Name the Beatles: **Ringo Starr, John Lennon, Paul McCartney, and George Harrison**

9. Pogo met the enemy and "**he is us**!"

10. Sonny and **Cher**

11. "**Wonder Bread** builds strong bodies 12 ways."

12. "You'll wonder where the yellow went **when you brush your teeth with Pepsodent**."

13. "Hey kids, what time is it?" "**It's Howdy Doody Time**!"

14. "**Brylcreem**—a little dab'll do ya!"

15. "**Hallmark Cards**—when you care enough to send the very best."

16. In "Frasier," Marty's dog is named **Eddie**.

17. "What's in your wallet?" **Capital One**

18. "M-I-C-**K-E-Y M-O-U-S-E**"

19. "It's the real thing—**Coca-Cola**."

20. "Good to the last drop: **Maxwell House Coffee**."

21. "Let **Hertz** put you in the driver's seat."

22. "Just the facts, ma'am," said **Joe Friday**. ("Dragnet" TV series)

23. "See the USA in your **Chevrolet**."

24. **Heinz**—57 varieties

25. "Fly the friendly skies."—**United Airlines**

When I Was a Kid . . .

Materials

None

Time

10 to 20 minutes

Procedure

Invite members of the group to think back to their childhood days. While in groups of three or four, ask them to share a memory (two, if time permits) of an experience or event that took place during their youth. Experiences could include family outings, school-day recollections, family pets, a special doll or toy, and so forth. Ask them to bring to mind as many descriptive and vivid details as possible. After a few minutes, ask if anyone would care to share his or her memory with the entire audience.

Discussion Questions

1. When was the last time you even thought of this experience or event?
2. Were you surprised at how fast the bits and pieces of the memories came back?
3. Did you have a vivid picture or clear details of this experience or event?
4. Memories are held in our long-term storage banks because they, in some way, have value. Are you aware of the value of the memories you recalled?
5. By learning about another person's experience, do you have a greater appreciation for him or her?

6

Adult Learning: Help Your Brain Adapt to Changing Situations

Learning is not compulsory . . . neither is survival.

—W. Edwards Deming

Chapter Highlights

You'll learn some basic principles of how adults learn best and how these laws underscore the importance of getting them involved in your programs. You'll also find some practical ideas on working with Gen X and Gen Y attendees.

By definition, learning is "a change of behavior because of some experience." It is the acquisition of knowledge or skills. In fact, you could say that learning literally *means* change.

While for many of us change may be a pleasant and even sought-after commodity, it is important to realize that for some of your attendees change is very difficult or even uncomfortable. Should you doubt this even for a moment, try the oft-used exercise of simply crossing your arms in front of yourself. Then, without looking down, ask yourself which arm is on top. Then, very quickly, unfold your arms and refold them so that the other arm is on top. Simple? Perhaps so, but try this in a group and watch the results. You will certainly find some awkwardness and even laughter as people see that such a simple physical change can be difficult.

The point? Well, if simple physical change is awkward or doesn't feel right, how much truer will that be for psychological change? We rest our case!

This chapter will explore some recent studies about how the brain works in gathering new information and how you can apply this knowledge to your own learning and teaching activities. You will learn *why* most people attend learning conferences and *how* you can make those meetings more effective.

We'll also delve into a few select principles and theories of adult learning and show their practical implications for your everyday activities.

You'll also review some recent research identifying different learning styles and how we all need to adapt our own delivery styles to make the most of each of these interactions. So whether it's a crowd of Boomers, Gen X-ers, Gen Y-ers (also known as Millennials)—or any other specially identified group—you'll have the tools and techniques to address these audiences effectively.

One of the most interesting aspects of the brain is its capacity to adapt itself to new and ever-changing situations. In this chapter you'll find cutting-edge research, but more important, methods and ideas to bring this research into your work. Let's get started.

Effective Meetings

So, what makes for an effective meeting? What goes into an excellent training session? What are the ingredients of a superb keynote or workshop presentation?

Today, more than ever before, the need for cost-effective meetings that show a solid ROI (return on investment) is critical. With time becoming more and more the currency of the 21st century, it is imperative that each of us understand the importance of having clearly defined objectives, addressing real and important issues, offering relevant and state-of-the-art information and content, and, oh, yes, ensuring that attendees leave the meeting feeling good about their experience!

The poet Maya Angelou said it well when she suggested that "people will forget what you said, they will forget what you did, but they will never forget how you made them feel."

Why People Attend Meetings

What if you planned a meeting and nobody came?

Well, without question, if you're the manager and you call a meeting for next Thursday at 10:00 A.M., everyone invited will be there. While that may be a given in the corporate world, such attendance is not necessarily the case when it comes to association meetings, public seminars, or even voluntarily attended training or educational programs.

So the question "Why attend meetings?" is a genuine one. Futurist Alvin Toffler suggests that people come to meetings for a variety of reasons:

- **Information:** The attendees of today are quite different from their counterparts of even a few years ago. They are younger, more sophisticated, better educated, and hungry for information. They want to learn new content, new concepts, and skills that will help them today and tomorrow—not five years from now!

- **Networking:** Not surprisingly, we find that many people choose to attend meetings and conferences for the networking, the camaraderie, and the overall collegiality they will find among their fellow attendees. Perhaps they just want to share experiences or "war stories" with their counterparts from around the country—or, these days, even around the world. Whatever the reason, there are many of us who attend meetings just to see old friends and make new ones.
- **Recreation:** "All work and no play. . . ." That's right; some people attend meetings just for the fun of it! This "fun," of course, may take a variety of forms, from golf tournaments to team-building activities to social events and more. Whatever the case, experienced facilitators understand the importance of building time into the program for these activities.

Theories of Adult Learning

In the past few years much attention has been given to the field of adult learning. Let's take a look at a few ideas that will be helpful for you and your attendees for your next meeting. Hundreds, if not thousands, of studies have investigated how the learning process takes place. You have already learned much about this in the previous chapters on the brain, attention, and memory. For example, an older adult would have a learning style considerably different from his or her younger counterparts. Younger audiences (who may well have grown up on Barney, "Sesame Street," and the like) may rightfully believe that learning should be couched in entertaining as well as informative methods. They know that learning can be fun, and studies have supported this very premise. And just for the record, that premise holds true for most any age.

The Learning Organization

Dr. Peter Senge of MIT, in a landmark book called *The Fifth Discipline*, gave the world of learning an incredible gift when he described what he called a "learning organization." He taught CEOs around the globe what learning is really all about in the corporate arena.

His definition is as follows: "Learning organizations are organizations where people continually expand their capacity to create the results they really desire . . . and where people are continually learning how to learn together."

Simple words, but they carry an enormous message for all of us.

While a learning disability is an unfortunate thing in a person, a "learning disability" can also be a tragic thing in the corporate world. Unless we have a way to capture and retain corporate culture over time, past history and learning can fall by the wayside—dooming us to make the same mistakes over and over. Luckily, there are a number of ways companies and other groups can strive to create a learning organization. For example, even something as simple as a lending library in the break room, with books and tapes in it, can help build the learning organization. Group meetings discussing a current business book of relevance might be another step toward a learning organization. The basic foundation of these organizations is that "all of us together are smarter than any one of us, and we can and should learn together."

Dr. Senge goes on to list the characteristics of a learning organization as follows:

1. It allows for both individual and organizational learning.
2. The focus is on adaptability and creativity.
3. The organization has a clear and well-defined vision.
4. It makes effective use of teams.
5. It displays a strong corporate (leadership) commitment.

Shifting Paradigms

As we review the changes in the working world since the shift to the knowledge economy, from the agricultural and industrial past, several points stand out. For instance:

1. The rigidity necessary in the "old days" has been replaced with a culture of change and flexibility.
2. The top-down pyramidal style of leadership has given way to a more horizontal structure.
3. The role of the autocrat is being supplanted by that of the empowering leader.
4. The status quo now searches for continuous improvement.

Pedagogy vs. Andragogy

Don't let the words scare you! The late Dr. Malcolm Knowles, a respected author and professor in the field of adult learning, coined the word *andragogy* some years back to differentiate how we learn as adults from how we learn as children (pedagogy). The basic thrust of andragogy is simply that adults differ in their learning styles and thus should not be subjected to the same pedantic teaching methods used with kids. (By the way, it would be nice if some of our current college professors understood and practiced this very simple truth!)

In other words, we can't use the same methodologies in working with our adult audiences as we ourselves may have been subjected to in our early learning activities.

Let's take a quick look at what andragogy purports to ensure. The four basic steps are so simple that it's a wonder they have not been embraced by the entire cadre of teachers, speakers, and HRDers.

1. **Adults are adults and don't want to be treated like a bunch of kids.** Wow—how's that for a novel suggestion? As obvious as this statement is, we see far too many colleagues who just don't seem to get it.

   Just for the fun of it, think back to the last meeting you attended, or perhaps the speaker at your last conference. Did you feel like you were addressed as an adult? If not, you already get the point.

   All too often, it seems, we find ourselves in situations like this, where we feel as though we're being talked down to. We are adults, and we have every right to be treated as such.

2. **Adults have more experience.** Your attendees have both life and work experience. This should be obvious, so why do we violate this principle by not acknowledging and capitalizing on this wealth of experience?

   Even if you're presenting a topic that may involve material new to your audiences, don't forget that people want to get involved. It's the very essence of experiential learning! Remember there's a world of learning out there, and your attendees may very well have experience or even expertise in a number of areas.

3. **There must be a readiness to learn.** We all know that motivation is an internal activity and you really can't force-feed the learning

process. But certainly times of day and even days of the week, at least, have implications for learning.

You've already learned that the brain functions better at certain times than others. For instance, most of us tend to learn better in the morning hours. On the other hand, a lot of our attendees may take a mental (or, heaven forbid, a physical!) siesta right after the lunch hour. Here, of course, is where the use of involvement techniques is critical.

4. **Keep it real.** While in many cases we build from theory, the best bet is always to keep the content as practical and relevant as possible. The more our participants can see connectivity between our content and their real-world jobs and activities, the more viable and effective the program is for them.

Remember that the more practical the information, the more likely they'll be transferring that training information into their long-term storage banks.

Laws of Adult Learning

Rather than recite a litany of these "laws of adult learning," let's look at just a few that have the most direct implications—and *applications*—for presenting our information.

Learning

Let's revisit what we mean by *learning*. We're referring here to the knowledge, skills, and attitudes that are obtained by study, observation, or emulation. Learning is simply the art of acquiring these skills. This change of behavior is what learning is all about.

Most learning theorists suggest that learning is indeed a lifelong process. It's self-development through activity. While nonassociative learning may play a role, the real key is experiential learning. The era of the "talking head" is dead, as well it should be. No one—especially our Gen X–ers and Gen Y–ers/Millennials—want to be talked at. They want an active role in their own learning activities.

Let's look at a few learning principles that you can put to use today.

1. **Law of Effect:** Essentially this rule suggests that people learn best in pleasant surroundings. (Parenthetically, may we add that people also "work" best in pleasant surroundings!) The importance of climate-setting activities, for example, is underscored when we realize that they serve to help individuals connect more easily with others. This sense of connection promotes a comfortable environment—hence, more pleasant surroundings.

   Think back to a recent situation when you walked into a room and didn't know anyone. How'd you feel? We all realize the impact a first impression can have. How do you suppose first-timers to your association or other group meeting feel as they walk in and don't know anyone? The point is obvious. Make certain that you have greeters or some way to make people feel welcome. Take a lesson from Walmart!

   Whether it's a large-scale convention or a small training program, if the Law of Effect is not working for you, it's probably working against you.

   Clearly, a well-set room with spacious seating is helpful. But even here, many of our meeting planner colleagues forget that the familiar room set with theater seating may not be the best. Even for larger groups, use a variety of room setups. Those long, straight rows clearly inhibit good eye contact with others—and may even cause neck strain after a long day of sitting. Consider using some variation of a more circular style. It's more comfortable and allows for a more casual atmosphere.

   Incidentally, for large-scale conferences, make sure the first rows of seating are fairly close to the stage. Speakers always lament the loss of energy in a room if the first row is a mile away.

   Music can also play a powerful role. Think of a movie or TV show you saw in the last few days. Think back to how the use of music can create a mood or atmosphere. So, too, can music aid materially in setting a climate. However, one caveat: make certain that if you *do* use music, it's appropriate for public use. Always check with legal counsel and with ASCAP (American Society of Composers, Authors and Publishers) and BMI (Broadcast Music, Inc.) to make sure that license agreements are in place.

2. **Law of Exercise:** You may be the best speaker or trainer around, but if you don't get the audience involved, you're missing the point. In fact, the noted educational theorist John Dewey made that forceful point many years ago when he said, "People learn best by doing."

   It is a proven fact that people retain more—in both short- and long-term memory—when they are actively involved in some part of the program. Retention is clearly best with some kind of involvement.

3. **Law of Readiness:** This principle relates to motivation and the internal desire people have to do the right thing. Regardless of how dynamic your presentation is, if your attendees are not ready, willing, and able to learn or participate, those efforts will miss their target. This often relates to time of day, day of week, etc., as you've already read in Chapter 4, about attention.

   It is no secret to any experienced meeting professional that most people may be a bit tired after that heavy lunch or long-winded speaker. Ensure that your facilitators understand that people will learn more readily when the need is more apparent. And make certain that the material they're presenting is relevant, timely, and important. In this way, you're bound to have better attention and results.

4. **Law of Association:** Picture a child on the floor playing with a bunch of building blocks. In all likelihood, this youngster places one block on top of another, then another on top of that, and so on, until he or she builds something. In a sense, learning is like that for many (but not all) of us. We go from the known to the unknown in short, manageable steps.

   In other words, we move from the old to the new knowledge a bit at a time, slowly bringing about new concepts, attitudes, etc. For most of us, it's a sequential, methodical process.

   However, it is important to note that this easy procedure—A to B to C—may not hold true for all learners. In particular, our Gen X and Gen Y audiences are skilled at multiswitching and are just as comfortable going from point A over to point J and then perhaps back to point D and so on. In other words, their learning style is quite different, so make sure your methods and techniques take this into consideration. Unless you acknowledge these various styles, you're going to lose your group in a hurry.

Generational Learning Styles

As you've already learned, we all have differing styles of learning. The old "one size fits all" approach doesn't fly with today's audiences—especially our Gen X–ers and Gen Y–ers.

So let's look at the various generations you have in your programs. Note that while we tend to distinguish these groupings by year of birth, there really is no clear-cut definition or demarcation. In other words, we all may tend to exhibit the qualities and characteristics of a differing age group at various times. That's what life is all about.

- **The "Mature" Generation**—those born before the mid-1940s. Obviously, many of these folks are already retired and not working, but there are still many who are in the workforce—perhaps on a part-time basis. (Been to a Walmart lately?) Typically, they are seen as dedicated, hard workers, loyal and respectful—and both thrifty and patriotic.
- **Baby Boomers**—usually identified as those born between 1946 and 1963. They number more than 70 million. They are career oriented and seek to build on relationships and results. They are seen as energetic, with strong values and ethics, and have high expectations for themselves and their colleagues. When working with Boomers, check their comfort level with technology before embarking on new projects. They'll appreciate the value of being a team member and make meaningful contributions. Even though they are a competitive breed, they are generally very respectful of their coworkers. Let them do it their way and be careful not to hover too much in any task.
- **Gen X or The Gen X–ers**—those born between 1964 and 1977. Because many grew up with single parents, they are often referred to as the "latchkey generation." They are quite comfortable with the latest gadgets and are extremely tech-savvy. Although they may tend to resist the formal structure and atmosphere of many organizations, they have a balanced work ethic. They will be most impressed by the

character of their leaders, so don't expect respect just because you carry a title. You'll need to prove it to them through your actions—not your words. They number around 45 million. They may seem blunt in their styles of communication, however, they just want to have fun in their everyday work and social activities.

- **The Millennials or Gen Y**—The joke "Generation Why?" says it all. However, somewhat contrary to popular belief, the Gen Y–er is actually polite and respects authority. However, much like their Gen X counterparts, they accord that respect to performance, not position. Also numbering around 70 million, they are multiswitching oriented and confident in themselves and their work. Born from 1978 to 2000, they know technology inside out. They demand interactivity in their work and learning activities. They crave challenges and like to work in teams.

So, here's the 64-million-dollar question: How do we and our colleagues deal with all these learning style differences in our programs?

As supervisors, managers, trainers, facilitators, speakers, and meeting planners, how can we ensure that we're meeting the needs of all these diverse groups? First, and most important, by simply knowing and acknowledging their learning and work style differences, you're already one step ahead of most.

Remember, regardless of the differing age groups in your meetings, the era of the "talking head" is dead. *No one* wants to listen to another boring speaker. Recognize that we all have short attention spans, so your typical 60- or 90-minute module is far too long without their engagement and involvement.

As you've already learned, you need to incorporate some kind of physical or mental activity every 5 to 10 minutes to retain their interest.

And don't forget to allow plenty of networking time—especially for large-scale conferences or meetings. Consider stretching that typical 15-minute break to 20 or 30 minutes. Why is this important? Besides the obvious, it allows more time for calls back to the office and checking BlackBerrys and text messages.

Also, if your program is one that involves concurrent sessions, it allows a time cushion for situations in which the previous speaker/facilitator goes over his or her allotted time. Finally, it allows more time for social networking, which is important no matter what your generation.

Ready, Set, Action

Involve your participants. Take the focus off yourself and put it on them. Find creative ways to get them involved. That is precisely what this book is all about.

The desire for action is one of the basic desires within all of us—and encouraging team members to take an active role not only meets this desire but is highly energizing and motivating. Let them shine by capitalizing on their expertise and experience.

As we've already suggested, today's meeting attendees are younger, smarter, far more sophisticated, and want to be entertained as well as taught. Until we recognize that different people have different learning styles, we're simply doing an injustice to our participants. And one thing we all have in common is that we all want meetings to be relevant and timely and to make good use of our time. So make sure your meetings are fast-paced, fun, and information-packed. That's a big order, but it's a necessary one!

Sooo, Howyadune? (Verbal Feedback Version)

OBJECTIVES
- To summarize at the meeting's midpoint
- To identify what participants are gleaning from the new concepts or learning

Materials

None

Time

15 to 20 minutes

Procedure

About 10 to 15 minutes prior to the morning and/or afternoon break, ask group members to partner with a new friend or colleague and quickly ask one another, "What new concepts or ideas have you learned so far?" Allow two or three minutes for discussion and then ask each two-person team to join with another two-person team, forming new groups of four people each. Then request that they again compare and share what others have learned. Then each subgroup is asked to report back to the entire group, sharing one or two key concepts or ideas they have learned.

Tip

This exercise is intended for half-day or longer programs.

Discussion Questions

1. As you reviewed your notes or memory, did one or two things jump out at you?

2. As you discussed your own learning points with your colleague(s), did you find they suggested totally different ideas?

3. Did any of you find your partner(s) jotted down an idea that wasn't even discussed in the session?

4. How could you use this activity at your office or work site?

Sooo, Howyadune?
(Visual Feedback Version)

OBJECTIVES
- To summarize at the meeting's midpoint
- To identify what participants are gleaning from the new concepts or learning

Materials

Copies of the Sooo, Howyadune? handout (provided)

Time

15 to 20 minutes

Procedure

About 10 to 15 minutes prior to the morning and/or afternoon break, ask group members to consider what new concepts or ideas they have learned so far. Explain that you will be inviting them to review and record a few concepts or ideas from the workshop/meeting, putting them on paper—not just listing them, but documenting them in a more creative manner. Give each participant the handout. Explain that they are to turn the doodles into images, stories, or concepts that represent what they have learned. If necessary, allow them to use any notes they might have taken during the workshop to prompt their memory. Be sure to let them know that artistic talent is not necessary. This is simply a fun and playful way to stimulate and enhance the memory process. Allow five to seven minutes and then ask participants to partner with another person and share their restructured doodles.

Tip

This exercise is intended for half-day or longer programs.

Discussion Questions

1. As you reviewed your notes or memory, did one or two things jump out at you?

2. As you discussed your own learning points with your colleague(s), did you find they suggested totally different ideas?

3. Did any of you find your partner(s) doodled an idea that wasn't even discussed in the session?

4. How could you use this activity at your office or work site?

Sooo, Howyadune?
(Visual Feedback Version)

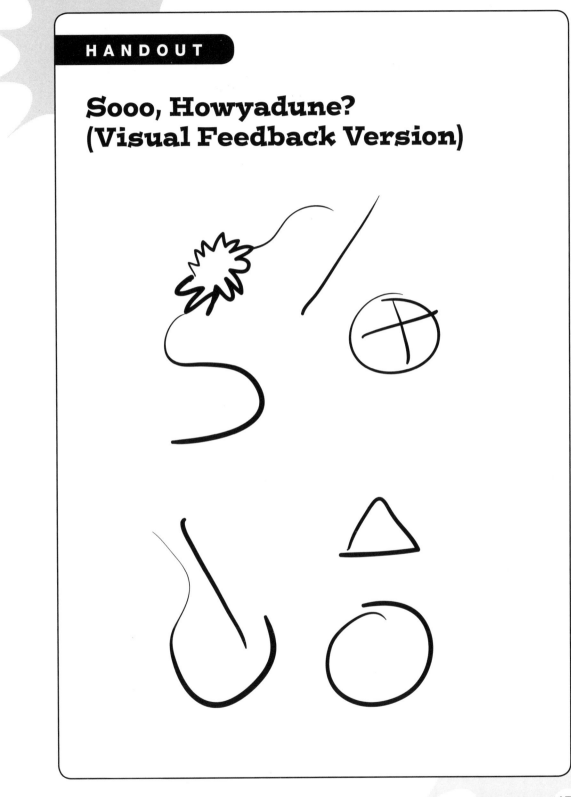

I Wish, I Wish

OBJECTIVE
- To assist in identifying potential problem areas in an organization

Materials

None

Time

10 to 15 minutes

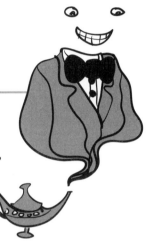

Procedure

To be used when doing personal interviews, either formal or informal, with coworkers. Ask if they have a wish list for their jobs. Ask them, if they could change anything about their jobs, what would it be?

Make notes during the discussion and continue as necessary to uncover—or discover—those areas that might be in need of immediate attention or concern.

Tip

This activity must be done in an atmosphere of trust and openness. Make sure participants realize this is not a "witch hunt" but rather a sincere effort to learn how these items might be improved. Form groups of three or fewer.

Discussion Questions

1. What is it that you like best about your job?
2. If you were king or queen for the day, what would you change in your company? How about your job?
3. What can we do to make your job easier? More productive?
4. What additional resources might you need?

The Law of Effect

Materials

Paper, pens

Time

10 to 15 minutes

Procedure

As was explained earlier in the chapter, the Law of Effect states that "people learn best in pleasant surroundings." Remind the group that this law is not only important in the learning environment but is also applicable in everyday situations, both personal and professional.

Divide the group into teams of three or four attendees. Ask participants to share with their teammates a recent situation at work when a manager, supervisor, or coworker paid them a compliment regarding their work or performance. After a few minutes, request that they now describe a situation when they gave a compliment to one of their colleagues. Finally, ask them to discuss how this law can be used with their own families and in social situations.

Discussion Questions

1. When was the last time you were given a minute of praise by a manager or supervisor? Tell us about it.
2. When was the last time you gave praise to one of your coworkers? How about your supervisors? Tell us about it.
3. Why do you think some of our colleagues fail to recognize that this law has universal applications?
4. Can you see applications for this when you're a customer in a store or restaurant? Any stories you'd like to share?

Actions Speak Louder than Words

- To demonstrate that "Actions speak louder than words!"

Materials

None

Time

1 minute

Procedure

We've all heard the saying "Actions speak louder than words." Tell the group you're about to demonstrate that to them.

Tell the participants to extend their right arm out to the right side of their body parallel to the floor (as you do the same thing). Ask them to then make a circle with their thumb and forefinger, as they continue to hold their arm out—as you demonstrate.

Then, as you quickly bring your circled thumb and forefinger to your **cheek**, tell the group to quickly bring their thumb and forefinger to their **chin**. (Thus you have instructed them to do something other than what you are demonstrating to them.)

Watch the results. Most of the group will dutifully follow your lead as they see you bring your thumb and forefinger to your cheek.

After a second—and as some of the people are laughing—simply say "Whoops, this is the cheek, not the chin! Don't do as I do; do as I say. Actions speak louder than words."

Discussion Questions

1. Many of you responded to my physical actions rather than my verbal instructions. Were you aware that they differed?

2. For those of you who were aware of the contradiction in my verbal instruction versus my behavior—which did you follow and why? Did you look to your colleagues to see what they were doing?

3. "Don't do as I do, do as I say." Have you experienced situations like this on the job?

4. What are some strategies you have found helpful in dealing with such situations?

Instant Experts

OBJECTIVE

- To illustrate that all of us are smarter than any one of us by engaging in a fun group activity

Materials

Flip chart, markers, paper, pens

Time

20 to 25 minutes

Procedure

Remind participants that learning takes place in both individual and group settings. Read aloud this definition of *learning organizations*: "organizations where people continually expand their capacity to create the results they really desire— and where people are continually learning how to learn together."

On a PowerPoint slide or flip chart, list several topics, such as "Customer Service," "Improving Functions of the Brain," "IQ vs. EQ," or any other topics of interest. Form teams of five or six and randomly assign a topic to each team. Explain that this is going to be a two-step process. First, they are to gather as much information as possible in reference to their flip chart topic from their immediate team members. Second, they are to interview members of other teams to glean additional information. Each team must interview at least three other teams in an effort to gather additional information. After 10 minutes of information collection, teams will be asked to reassemble and spend 5 minutes preparing their presentation, which will be delivered to the entire group.

Discussion Questions

1. How did your team develop its strategy for gathering information?

2. Were you surprised to learn that others had expertise in your assigned topic?

3. Could you use the same approach in capturing some history or information from others at your office?

Dealing with Change

Materials

Copies of Dealing with Change handout (provided)

Time

15 to 20 minutes

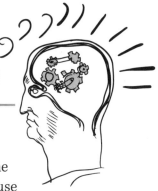

Procedure

Acknowledge that change is the "name of the game" for all of us. We often, however, fail to use our gained wisdom as a coping tool for future experiences. Give each participant a copy of the Dealing with Change handout and form teams of three or four. Ask participants to think of a recent change they've experienced at their workplace. Allow participants 2 to 3 minutes to complete the form and then ask them to share their experiences with the others on their team. After 5 to 10 minutes of discussion, ask for volunteers to share their story with the other teams.

Discussion Questions

1. Did most of you think of a recent example of a change that affected you, either personally or professionally?
2. For the most part, did you find that many of you and your coworkers tended to resist it initially?
3. As you discussed the last question on the handout (What would have made it easier?), how many agreed that communication—or, more likely, a lack of it—was the main culprit?
4. What were some other factors?

Dealing with Change

Please take a moment and review this worksheet. Think of a recent situation—
either on the job or even a personal situation—in which you were involved. This
can include situations when you were the initiator, the person who was charged
with carrying out the directive, or the person on the receiving end of things.

1. List one or two changes that you've experienced recently:

_____

_____

2. Was this change resisted? If so, how did this resistance show up?

_____

_____

3. Why did you resist the change? Or why not?

_____

_____

4. Looking back on the situation, what do you think would have made that
change experience either easier to sell or to get buy-in on?

_____

_____

7

He Said, She Said: Explore Gender Differences in Learning

The basic discovery about any people is the discovery of the relationship between its men and women.

—Pearl S. Buck

Chapter Highlights

This chapter provides an overview of some of the major structural and functional differences in the brains of males and females and how these differences show up in our lives.

For eons we've acknowledged, contemplated, and occasionally even celebrated the fact that males and females are different—no surprise here.

Yet until the late 1980s scientists tended to focus on exploring mainly the workings of the male brain, presuming that the brains of men and women were alike (except during a woman's pregnancy). Of course, they had some valid rationale for focusing primarily on the study of the male brain. One major reason was that before the capabilities of the noninvasive brain imaging technologies, men's brains were in greater supply. Earlier neuronatomy (exploration of the workings of the brain) utilized the brains of soldiers who had lost their lives in battle.

More recently, thanks to cutting-edge brain imaging technologies, researchers have been able to view *in real time* the intriguing activity of both the male and female brain. Truly one of the most fascinating realizations is that when an identical task is assigned to both males and females, different areas in their brains become activated. According to Louann Brizendine, M.D., in her book *The Female Brain*, "Granted, the genetic coding of the male and female brain may be 99 percent the same, but that one percent influences every single cell in our bodies—from the nerves that register pleasure and pain to the neurons that transmit perception, thoughts, feelings and emotions."

So, apparently, there is no unisex approach to brain chemistry (except during the first eight weeks of conception). Generally, if you give a little girl a truck to play with, she'll cuddle it, rock, it, and gently sing it to sleep. Give a little boy a doll, and if the size is right (or even if it's not), it will soon be finding its way through the nearest basketball hoop or be used to dig ditches, construct roadways, and even fight battles. At this early stage in life, she's already into relationships and he's into objects and spatial-mechanical principles. We're wired this way! And this wiring, coupled with our hormonal differences and environmental factors, forms the basis for the gap between male and female attitudes, beliefs, preferences, and behaviors.

According to husband and wife authors Barbara and Allan Pease, in their entertaining but scientific book entitled *Why Men Don't Listen and Women Can't Read Maps,* "... men and women are different. Not better or worse—just different. Society today is determined to believe that men and women possess exactly the same set of skills, aptitudes, and potentials— just as science, ironically, is beginning to prove that they are completely different. Men and women evolved differently because they had to. Men hunted, women gathered. Men protected and women nurtured. As a result, their bodies and brains evolved in completely different ways."

We're not suggesting or supporting superiority or inferiority—we're simply recognizing and appreciating areas of uniqueness.

Structural Differences

The brain's wiring, which ultimately dictates the differences between male and female brains, actually begins around eight weeks after conception. Let's take a short step back to review some of your ninth-grade biology basics (don't panic; it'll be brief). If the male sperm that fertilizes the female egg carries an X chromosome, a baby girl will be born, and if the sperm carries a Y chromosome (signaling a release of testosterone), we'll have a baby boy.

However, according to Dr. Brizendine, "Until eight weeks old, every fetal brain looks female—female is nature's default gender setting. A huge testosterone surge beginning in the eighth week will turn this unisex brain male by killing off some cells in the communication centers and growing more cells in the sex and aggression centers. If the testosterone surge doesn't happen, the female brain continues to grow unperturbed."

The consequences of this eight-week event (testosterone or no testosterone) will in some manner affect every biological, physiological, hormonal, psychological, and chemical process destined for this fetus.

Let's take a closer look at how this initial event translates into structural differences within the male and female brain. Although Michael Gurian, author of *What Could He Be Thinking?,* believes there are almost 100 structural differences in the male and female brains, we will address only a very few—those that appear to be most obvious.

The male brain is approximately 8 to 15 percent larger than the female brain and contains a higher percentage of white matter (connections between the information-processing centers). The female brain contains more gray matter (information-processing centers) and a thicker/heavier corpus callosum (the cable or communication connection between the left and right hemispheres).

In males, the parietal cortex, involved in spatial perception, is larger than in women. The male also possesses a larger amygdala, which deals with emotionally arousing stimuli (increased heart rate and adrenaline flow). The frontal cortex (higher cognitive functions) is larger in women, as is the limbic system (responsible for emotional responses—not surprised, are you?).

Although the female brain is smaller, women and men have the same number of brain cells. It seems, according to Dr. Louann Brizendine, that the difference in the size can be attributed to the fact that the cells in a female brain are more tightly packed. Table 7.1 charts some of the basic structural and physiological differences within the male and female brain.

Of course, in real life the characteristics of males and females overlap. Also, one must also take into consideration the role of social influences and cultural conditioning when assigning specific gender traits. Most important, research relates to the law of averages. Individuals, however, *do not* obey the law of averages!

Functional Differences

In this section we will identify some of the major functional differences or distinctions in the male and female and how they manifest in real life (see Table 7.2). Discussing these dissimilarities will allow us to appreciate how they affect our everyday behaviors and interactions between the sexes. Again, we stress that these differences in traits are based on averages. Many masculine and feminine social behaviors are learned. To wit, we all know many males who are nurturing and just as many females who hate to be wrong.

TABLE 7.1	Basic Structural Differences Between the Male and Female Brain	
	FEMALES	**MALES**
Brain Size	Smaller—2⅔ pounds (equal in size to male brain by middle age)	Bigger—3 pounds (shrinks faster than in females from adolescence on)
Gray Matter (cell bodies of the information-processing center)	Higher percentage than males with same amount in both hemispheres	Lower percentage than females, with more in left hemisphere than right
White Matter (nerve fibers—networking between information centers)	Lower percentage than males	Higher percentage than females
Corpus Callosum (nerve fibers allowing communication between the two hemispheres)	Larger and thicker than in males	Smaller and thinner than in females
Language Area (speech and context of language)	Main areas in left hemisphere, with additional processing areas in right hemisphere; greater density of neurons in language area than in males	Located almost exclusively in left hemisphere; less density of neurons in language area than females
Amygdala (responds to emotional stimulation)	Grows slower in teenage girls than boys, and final size is smaller than in males; only the left amygdala activated by emotional stimulation; activation linked to verbal response areas	Grows faster in teenage boys than in girls, and final size is larger than in females; only right amygdala activated by emotional stimulation; activation linked to motor/physical response areas
Hippocampus (center for learning, memory formation and consolidation)	Grows faster in teenage girls than in boys, and final size is larger than in males	Grows slower in teenage boys than in girls, and final size is smaller than in females

Adapted from *How The Brain Learns* by David A. Sousa, 2006, pg. 173.

Vision

Females have much greater visual capabilities than males. Visual perception in females engages both hemispheres, while in males only the right hemisphere is activated. Females are especially skilled in peripheral vision. They are apt to have up to 180 degrees of peripheral vision, which means

TABLE 7.2	Functional Differences in Males and Females	
FEMALES	**MALES**
Interrupt to clarify or support others	Interrupt to introduce new information
Possess a longer attention span	Possess a shorter attention span
Form informal organizations	Form hierarchical organizations
Take more interest in people	Take more interest in objects
Are slower to anger	Are easier to anger
Listen emotively	Listen literally
Involve their language center to solve math problems	Use only left hemisphere to solve math problems
Prefer sweet flavors—chocolate lovers	Prefer salty tastes—beer lovers
Require less space	Require more space
Use more eye contact	Use less eye contact
More sensitive to touch	Less sensitive to touch
React to pain more quickly	React to pain slowly
Cope with long-term pain better	Cope with long-term pain less well
Don't mind making mistakes	Hate to be wrong
Look to cooperate	Look to compete
Discuss relationships	Discuss things and activities
When stressed, talk to others	When stressed, talk to themselves
Openly reveal their emotions	Conceal their emotions
Extremely sensitive skin	Relatively thick and insensitive skin

that they can see events that are occurring around them without even turning their heads. This is why women are more likely to be involved in auto accidents where they are hit from the back or front (or while parallel parking) than from the side. Males have a narrow field of vision but are much better at distance vision, depth perception, and spatial abilities, which provide them with the "blinder effect," allowing them to focus in one direction only (like the TV screen!).

Although females' eyesight is superior at night and males are better at seeing in bright lights, women should still leave the night driving to men.

Males' distance vision capabilities coupled with their narrow field of focus make them a much safer bet for long-distance night driving.

When it comes to determining shades of colors, females have more cones (cells in the brain that handle color detection) and therefore tend to notice and describe colors in greater detail. A male may say he saw a blue jacket (a basic color), whereas a woman is likely to say that what she saw was a teal, aqua, turquoise, royal blue, navy blue, or iridescent blue jacket.

Women also excel at visual memory, facial recognition, and interpreting facial clues with respect to context. Men are often amazed at how a woman can scan a room full of people for a total of 10 seconds and then share with him the following:

Jack and Betty are having marital problems. (He looks over and thinks that they appear to be just fine to him.) Beth is pregnant, probably only about three weeks. (He thinks, How can anyone tell? It's too early.) Shannon is in love with her new boyfriend. (He notices that the boyfriend is not even anywhere in sight—this doesn't make sense).

Women have extraordinary sensory perception, coupled with a proficient means of rapid left-right hemispherical communication. They can quickly observe, assimilate, and integrate the incoming cues. They will then assess any contradictory information and then decipher the situation or event accordingly.

Hearing

Females may be better equipped to tune in to the tone, vocal nuances, volume, and pitch of sounds, but males are better equipped to pinpoint from which direction a sound has come.

Speaking (Communication)

Women excel at talking. Women communicate. Women discuss—they chat, they converse, they express themselves vocally—often! Women even think out loud . . . and they've had lots of practice. Females generally start talking before males—by age three, they have twice the vocabulary of their male counterparts, and their language comprehension is about 90 percent on average.

The female brain is beautifully designed to support endless communication. Her language and vocabulary functions are processed in both the right and left hemisphere, while in the male only the left hemisphere is activated. Brain scans show that women can talk and listen at the same time. It may not sound all that impressive, but it is—just think of how much more efficient conversations would be with this ability. During conversation, the speech centers of her left and right hemispheres and her hearing centers are all activated at the same time. Men's brains are not capable of performing this task. They can either speak or listen, but not both at once.

The male may not process language and vocabulary in both the left and right hemispheres like the female, but unlike her, he has very specific areas in his left hemisphere that focus strongly on vocabulary. He may not speak as often as the female, and certainly not as much, but when he does speak it tends to be "to the point."

Men think, and therefore speak, in literal terms. Their brains are compartmentalized, allowing them to deal with one thing at a time and then put it away to deal with the next issue at hand. The female brain, in contrast, has been referred to as the *superhighway*, with information traveling at warp speed back and forth across both hemispheres, allowing her to bring relationships and emotions into most every situation. Hence the following:

He says, "Honey, I noticed that there is a bare spot on the front lawn. I'll fix that when I finish my coffee."

That's it—a bare spot—needs to be fixed. Dan is functioning from one box—one compartmentalized idea.

She says, "Dan, why is it that everybody else always comes before me and my needs?"

Dan, says, "Whaat? I thought you'd be happy that I planned to fix the lawn!"

She replies, "Well, yes, but you didn't fix it very fast five years ago when it happened. And Chuck never helps you with any of your projects. And you never even finished making one airplane. I certainly hope that when Chrissy visits me next month you'll be a little more considerate of my feelings."

Dan may be stumped, but this conversation makes perfect sense to his wife, whose superhighway brain has just made a tour of numerous memories from the past, all of which were connected to emotions. Very different from the compartmentalized approach that Dan has taken.

This is the tour Dan's wife took:

Five years ago there was a bare spot in that same place, and for three weeks I asked him to fix it. I thought it made the whole front of the house look cheap. I had invited my girlfriend, Mary Helen, to visit, and she'd never seen our home. I wanted it to look nice. But, would he fix it? NO! Every weekend he had something else planned. His father wanted him to go fishing—and he doesn't even like fishing! Chuck wanted help fixing his car. Plus, Dan decided that he'd start a new hobby building little wooden airplanes, of all things—and had to attend the ONLY workshop that was being offered in the next six months. When Mary Helen arrived, the big ugly spot was there, so huge it might as well have been screeching at her saying, "Here I am! I'm an ugly, ugly, ugly bare spot. I represent how little Dan really cares about his wife." Yes, everybody and everything comes before me. And Chrissy's going to be visiting here next month—he'd better fix that spot in time.

Skills and Tasks

Because female and male brains are physically structured in different ways, and because at times they even use different areas of their brains to accomplish the very same task, it should come as no surprise that there would also be differences in capabilities when performing certain skills and tasks (see Table 7.3). In most every book and article written within the past few years addressing the topic of gender differences, you'll read something to the effect of "differences in abilities and skills do not translate to inequality. We're not suggesting or supporting superiority or inferiority— we're only recognizing and appreciating areas of uniqueness."

The purpose of distinguishing between men and women is not to further segregate the two sexes; rather, it's to encourage an awareness and appreciation for the uniqueness that each possesses. Only through recognition, understanding, and acceptance can we learn to respect and honor these differences and use that awareness to build foundations for healthy relationships.

TABLE 7.3	Gender Differences in Performing Skills and Tasks
WOMEN	**MEN**
General verbal abilities	General math reasoning
Visual memory	Auditory memory
Spelling	Spatial 3-D reasoning
Fluency of verbal production	Working vocabulary
Fine motor skills	Targeted skills
Remembering landmarks	Reading maps
Foreign languages	Playing chess
Reading body language	Problem-solving skills
Interpreting facial expressions	Better at habit formation
Computational tests	Better at reading blueprints
Better perception in red end of color spectrum	Better perception in blue end of color spectrum

Adapted from *Brain-Based Learning*, Eric Jensen, 2008, p. 34.

Brain Teaser #4

Materials
Copies of the Brain Teaser #4 handout
(provided)

Time
5 to 15 minutes

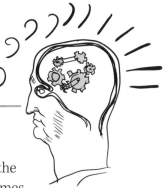

Procedure

Give each audience member a copy of the handout. Explain that each of the 16 frames or boxes in the quiz suggests a well-known slogan, phrase, or saying and that the task is to decipher the hidden message in each box. To get the exercise started and ensure that the group has a clear understanding of how the quiz works, provide an answer to any one of the frames. Allow participants two to three minutes to work the quiz on an individual basis. Then suggest that they pair up with a partner and see how many more frames they can solve together. Allow another two to three minutes. Then, starting with frame #1, begin soliciting answers from the group for each of the frames. If a response is fairly close to the "right" answer, simply paraphrase the answer to make it the correct one.

Discussion Questions

1. How many frames were you able to solve correctly on your own?
2. How many more when you worked with others?
3. When working with partners, did you come up with alternate answers?
4. Are you able to create some of these brain teasers yourself? Try one now. Is it easier solving a brain teaser or creating a brain teaser?

Brain Teaser #4

Decipher the hidden meaning of each box. Each of these describes a well-known saying or slogan.

1. KNOW LEDGE	**2.** H☺UR	**3.** STEP ꟼƎTꙄ ꟼƎTꙄ	**4.** RASINGININ
5. BALLO	**6.** C EXPLORATION	**7.** GOL	**8.** CHAMIRGE
9. C O N	**10.** U R B A N	**11.** MATS MATS MATS MATS	**12.** S K I N N Y
13. MY LI1111FE	**14.** brainer	**15.** W ☆ R S W ☆ R S W ☆ R S	**16.** tistitchme

Brain Teaser #4 Answers

1. Knowledge gap

2. Happy hour

3. One step forward, two steps backward

4. "Singin' in the rain"

5. Absentee ballot

6. Undersea exploration

7. Backlog

8. Am I in charge?

9. Condescending

10. Urban sprawl

11. Formats

12. Skinny-dipping

13. "For once in my life"

14. No brainer

15. *Star Wars*

16. Stitch in time

Male-Female Brains

OBJECTIVE
- To illustrate how men and women may process information differently

Materials

Copies of Table 7.2, Functional Differences in Males and Females

Time

15 to 20 minutes

Procedure

Based on the information in this chapter, it is clear that male and female brains are structured differently. This difference in structure translates to differences in the way males and females process information and, therefore, how we function or react to our environment. Form teams of four to six, preferably with an even mix of males and females. Review the differences shown in Table 7.2, "Functional Differences in Males and Females," on page 169, and request that teams discuss this list for their agreement or disagreement.

Discussion Questions

1. As you reviewed the male-female functional differences, did you discover some startling information?
2. As you discussed your reactions with your colleagues, did you feel/think the suggested differences were valid?
3. In working relationships, what have you learned that will enhance your understanding of one another?

Male-Female Perceptions

OBJECTIVE
- To increase awareness of and appreciation for functional male and female skills and abilities

Materials

Paper, pens, pencils, copies of Table 7.3, Gender Differences in Performing Skills and Tasks

Time

10 to 15 minutes

Procedure

Form teams of five to seven participants. Ask teams to list five to seven behaviors, traits, skills, or abilities that they perceive males, as opposed to females, excelling in. Then repeat for females. Explain that you're not suggesting or supporting superiority or inferiority—that we're simply recognizing and appreciating areas where we demonstrate our uniqueness. After they have listed five to seven traits for males and five to seven traits for females, distribute copies of Table 7.3, "Gender Differences in Performing Skills and Tasks," on page 173. Ask teams to compare their team lists with the results of the research shown in the chart. Have them discuss their findings.

Discussion Questions

1. Were the unique skills and abilities of the males versus females listed by your team members similar to those skills and abilities listed on the research chart?
2. If not, were you surprised? Do you disagree?
3. Are you offended by any of the items listed? If so, which ones?
4. Do you believe some skills and abilities are perceived as being positive or less than positive?

Circle of Inclusion

OBJECTIVE
- To demonstrate how our attitudes and intentions can affect how we approach, explore, understand, and appreciate differences in others

Materials

Flip chart paper and markers for each table; enough small prizes to award all participants on two teams (optional)

Time

20 to 30 minutes

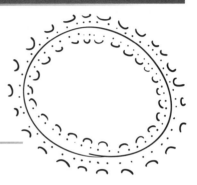

Procedure

We all recognize similarities and dissimilarities with those we encounter (at our place of work or in our relationships). We tend to identify similarities with others as positive experiences and dissimilarities and differences with others as less than positive experiences. When we acknowledge these dissimilarities/differences in others as being unique and distinctive characteristics, we become more accepting.

Divide the group into teams of five to seven participants. Ask each team to select a leader/scribe (if you need a neutral selection method, suggest that this person be chosen based on whose birth date is closest to today). Ask the leaders to draw a large circle on each of their flip chart papers. Explain that two tasks will follow and that the winning team for each will be awarded prizes, based on who has the most items listed. Task number one is to identify which points/items every single person on their team has in common—similar tastes, beliefs, experiences (example: everyone has a sister; everyone has visited Paris; everyone enjoys gourmet cooking)—and have leaders list these similarities as fast as they can inside the large circle. Allow four to five minutes. Now, for task number two, ask participants to identify as many dissimilarities as they can, as fast as they can. Have team leaders list these on the outside of their circles (example: four people on a team like spinach and one person does not). Allow another four to five minutes.

Tip
The larger the group, the longer the time required and the more challenging the execution.

Discussion Questions

1. Ask team leaders to report how many *similarities* were recorded and ask for two to three examples.

2. Identify the team that had the most similarities recorded and ask the leader to share the most unusual items listed. (Optional: award prizes to all members of this team.)

3. Ask team leaders to report how many dissimilarities were recorded and ask for two to three examples.

4. Identify the team that had the most dissimilarities recorded and ask the leader to share the most unusual items listed. (Optional: award prizes to all members of this team.)

5. Ask all participants which they found easier to accomplish—identifying the similarities or identifying the differences—and why they thought this to be the case.

6. Ask participants, "Do you think that because you had the opportunity to be rewarded for finding differences you tended to be eager to seek those differences and, consequently, excited when you found them?"

7. Ask if they are, in everyday life, as excited or accepting when they discover that others have different opinions/values/beliefs from theirs.

8. Why is it that we can be so open and excited about identifying differences when participating in this activity and not in our everyday life? Is it because of the allure of prizes, the delight in competition, or is there something else?

My, How You've Changed!

Materials

None

Time

5 to 10 minutes

Procedure

In discussing the elements of change, Dr. Ken Blanchard of *The One Minute Manager* fame shows us that experiencing change from a personal point of view helps us understand the concept of change on a professional level.

Ask the members of the group to stand and to find a new friend—someone they've not yet met or worked with. Ask them to introduce themselves to each other and then to simply take a moment to "study" the appearance of their new partner. After a moment, ask them to turn their backs to each other and, without their new friend being able to see them, change three things about their own appearance—switch their name tag to the other shoulder, put their watch on their other wrist, etc. Allow a minute or two and then ask them to face their partner again. Allow about two minutes to see if partners are able to identify all the changes that were made. Then ask that they take their seats to respond to the following questions.

Discussion Questions

1. When asked to change three things, how many of you found it difficult to change even three things? *(Lesson: when initiating or effecting change, don't try to do everything in one fell swoop—rather, take just one or two things and assimilate those before moving on.)*

2. When asked to change three things, how many of you almost instinctively took something off or took something away? *(Lesson: change doesn't have to be negative—it can be adding something rather than taking something away.)*

3. Now that you are seated comfortably as you were a few minutes ago, how many of you, right now, are exactly the same way you were—i.e. the name tag went back to the original shoulder, the tie got straightened, etc.? *(Lesson: Change takes time. You may "play my game" for a few minutes, but human behavior theory suggests it may take weeks or months before change is totally embraced.)*

Made to Stick

Procedure

In *Made to Stick,* by Chip and Dan Heath, the authors address the questions of why some ideas thrive while others die and how we improve the chances of worthy ideas. Their attention-getting book goes on to describe the methods to incorporate to ensure that an idea "sticks." These six simple and workable tips are what the authors believe all great ideas have in common for getting attention and favorable responses to our ideas:

1. Simplicity
2. Unexpectedness
3. Concreteness
4. Credibility
5. Emotions
6. Stories

Give each participant a copy of the handout and review the six principles listed on the sheet. Request that they select a project they are currently working on and write their idea or concept at the top of the worksheet. Allow participants 5 to 10 minutes, working individually, to apply as many of the six principles to their selected idea as possible. Then ask them to work with another colleague for even more ideas. Allow 5 to 10 more minutes.

Discussion Questions

1. How many of these principles did you use?

2. Do these questions spur further thinking on your part?

3. Would anyone care to tell us how they used this?

4. Would the same questions be applicable in other areas of your work—or even your personal life?

Made to Stick

In their bestselling book *Made to Stick*, authors Chip and Dan Heath suggest we use six basic principles for getting action on our ideas and positive feedback on our work projects.

Record your idea or concept:

_____

_____

Read the following principles and jot down any ideas that would materially assist you in selling your ideas to others.

1. **Simplicity:** What's the basic idea in its simplest form? What do you want others to remember?

_____

_____

2. **Unexpectedness:** Try something new and different. Surprise or jolt them. What's an outlandish idea that will capture their attention?

_____

_____

3. **Concreteness:** Offer them some solid ideas on your project. Give them some testimonials and other things they can latch on to and sell the benefits.

_____

_____

4. **Credibility:** Does it make sense in their eyes? Is it believable? Give them some arguments to show yours is the best way to approach the challenge.

_____

_____

5. **Emotions:** Remember, people often buy because of an emotional response, not necessarily based on rational thoughts. How does your idea hit them? Play on their emotions.

_____

_____

6. **Stories:** People love stories! Give them some examples of how your idea has worked in other situations. Illustrate it as much as possible.

_____

_____

8

Full Brain Fitness: Enhance and Enrich Brain Function

Your lifestyle choices and behaviors may influence brain shrinkage in old age. Basically, if you stay fit, you retain key regions of your brain involved in learning and memory.

—*Kirk I. Erickson, Ph.D.*

Chapter Highlights

This chapter provides an overview of some of the most recent "brain fitness" suggestions to nurture, nourish, and protect the priceless organ we call the brain.

Who doesn't want a stronger, healthier, more flexible body? For the last four decades, books and magazines have been crammed with information on what to eat and not eat to decrease body fat, increase lean body mass, and gain and maintain optimal weight. Body-enhancing equipment manufacturers continue to produce new devices to help us achieve a fit, firm, and attractive appearance. Vitamin, mineral, and supplement companies have warned of the many toxic substances we need to avoid, while promoting vitamins, minerals, and herbs. Pharmaceutical companies continue to develop drugs to heal our tissues, decrease our pain, and regrow our hair. All these products, programs, and developments have appeared in the marketplace based on the consumer's desire to preserve, protect, and enhance their bodies (or sometimes their image or just their vanity!)

Now, thanks to the dedication of our industrious scientific, medical, and health care specialists, we've been granted our wish for increased longevity. From 1900 to 2007, life expectancy has increased from 45 years to approximately 78 years. So now we must focus on adding quality to those years by caring for and protecting the precious organ that grows, shapes, and sustains all our human abilities.

Sadly, it has been predicted by some researchers that approximately 70 percent of all people may eventually face some decline in their cognitive abilities. However, others support a much more positive forecast for our brains' health. With the largest number ever (and still growing) of people over 65 years of age, there is a new imperative for researchers to better understand how to maintain a healthy brain—because we've come to the stark realization that an increased life span without an increased brain span is quite tragic.

Gifts to Give Your Brain

The following offers a summary of several "brain fitness" strategies (gifts to give your brain) based on the recommendations of the world's most prominent brain health care specialists. It is suggested that you not attempt too many changes at once. Sample some, experiment with some, amuse yourself with some—but whatever you do, nurture, nourish, engage, and expand your brain. Following even a few of these recommendations will increase the probability of your sporting a sharper, clearer, more alert, and more flexible brain. Join the brain fitness revolution!

Note: We recommend that you consult a qualified medical professional prior to beginning any new health care regime.

The Gift of Walking, Running, Skipping, Hopping, Jumping, Hiking

Physical exercise, we've long known, is good for the body. Now we realize that we have an additional motive for jumping on that treadmill or going for a brisk walk. It seems that boosting your cardiovascular activity also increases the number of capillaries in your brain. This, in turn, enhances blood flow and increases the amount of oxygen and glucose (brain food) delivered to the brain cells. According to Dr. John Medina, author of *Brain Rules*, "a lifetime of exercise can result in a sometimes astonishing elevation in cognitive performance, compared with those who are sedentary. Exercisers outperform couch potatoes in tests that measure long-term memory, reasoning, attention, problem-solving, and even so-called fluid-intelligence tasks." Research has shown that brisk walking three days a week can enhance your mental abilities by 15 percent.

It was discovered some time ago that the hippocampus (associated with memory and learning) shrinks as we age. However, a new study has revealed that individuals who are more physically fit tend to also have bigger hippocampi. The bigger the hippocampus, the better the spatial memory. According to Erickson, "This is really a clinically significant finding because it supports the notion that your lifestyle choices and behaviors may influence brain shrinkage in old

age. Basically, if you stay fit, you retain key regions of your brain involved in learning and memory."

In addition, physical activity regulates your appetite, reduces the risk of numerous types of cancer, improves your immune system, buffers against stress, and lowers the risk of heart disease, stroke, and diabetes. And there's more good news: exercise causes the release of the neurotransmitters (serotonin, dopamine, and norepinephrine) that have a powerful, positive effect on mood and on overall mental health. Performing just 30 minutes of aerobic exercise twice a week can decrease your risk of general dementia by 50 percent and reduce your risk of Alzheimer's by 60 percent.

All these potential benefits just from doing 30 minutes of cardiovascular exercise two to three times a week! So why not give your brain a lasting gift—go walk, run, skip, hop, and jump!

The Gift of Sleep

Sleep—it consumes approximately one-third of our entire lives, yet scientists are still undecided as to exactly *why* we sleep. Sleep study experts know that sleep is not an opportunity for our brains to take a siesta, since there is more synaptic activity  during sleep than when an individual is fully awake. In fact, it appears that the only time during the five stages of sleep that the brain does any resting at all is during the non-REM sleep cycle (only 20 percent of the total 90-minute sleep cycle). What researchers do agree on is that sleep seems to be a time to reorganize, encode, rearrange, and replay the stimuli we've been exposed to during our waking hours. Because information is encoded into your long-term memory during REM (rapid-eye movement) sleep, a good night's sleep can enhance the learning process appreciably. Conversely, this valuable memory storage process can be hampered with inadequate sleep.

Also impaired by inadequate sleep are attention, alertness (32 percent reduction of alertness with a 1½-hour loss of sleep), short-term memory, mood, logical reasoning, immune system, executive functioning, and motor skills (insufficient sleep doubles the risk of occupational injury). The possible long-term effects of sleep loss include high blood pressure, heart attack, heart failure, stroke, depression/mood disorders, mental impairment, relationship problems, and obesity.

How much sleep is an adequate amount? The answer to this question remains elusive. There appears to be no perfect *number* of sleep hours for the general masses. Your optimum sleep schedule should be a self-identifying process based on how you feel and how you function. Don't be surprised if your schedule or your personal sleep requirements change during your different life stages—this is a normal body/brain adjustment.

Need a nap? Good thing nap time isn't just for the little tykes. There may not be a universally accepted total number of hours we need to sleep each night, but when it comes to getting some shut-eye, there does exist one universal biological drive: the nap. Sometime during the midafternoon we all experience the longing to snooze. This *doze desire* is a product of our human evolution. Studies have shown that naps, anywhere from 15 to 45 minutes, can significantly increase productivity and cognitive performance. Based on the doze desire, you may want to rethink when to schedule that high-priced guest speaker or the meeting to meticulously review the budget.

Tips for a Healthy Night's Sleep

- Maintain a sleep schedule: Even sleeping an hour later on weekends can disrupt your internal clock and thus disturb your sleep cycle.
- Avoid alcohol close to bedtime: You may fall asleep easily but wake up numerous times throughout the night. Alcohol disrupts sleep patterns.
- Avoid caffeinated drinks before bedtime: It takes 14 hours for caffeine to leave the body. Caffeine increases the time needed to go to sleep, disrupts sleep, and decreases the duration of sleep.
- Avoid nicotine: It impairs sleep quality and inhibits the ability to sleep deeply.
- Quiet and dark: Bright lights and noise disrupt the sleep cycle. Use a night-light—and earplugs if necessary.
- Exercise: Finish your exercise at least 3 hours before bedtime.
- Don't watch the late evening news: News programs often lean toward negative reporting, and this type of stimulation before bedtime should be avoided.

- Develop a relaxing routine: This prepares the mind, body, and spirit for sleep—reading, a hot bath, or soothing music.
- Reserve your bedroom for S & S: sleep and sensuality—no TV!
- Don't discuss big problems with your spouse: Save the heavy discussions for another time.
- No pets in bed: Your pets have different sleep rhythms. Gift them with their own beds—and yourself with yours.
- Napping: DO IT, unless you have difficulty getting to sleep at night.
- No visible clock: Put the clock on the other side of the room and turn it away from you. Seeing the time brings you to an alert state.

The Gift of Balance and Harmony

Giving the gift of balance and harmony to your brain requires *nurturing* your brain—promoting, encouraging, and sustaining the health, development, and well-being of this vital organ. This balance and harmony, however, does not come effortlessly. In our harried culture, we must make a conscious and concerted effort to achieve balance and harmony. Stress, of course, is the most fierce and common adversary to the peace and tranquility that our bodies and brains crave.

Certainly not all stress is "bad" stress. Since the cave-dwelling days, our brains/bodies have been equipped with this unique and amazing automatic mechanism for responding to danger and peril—it's called our *stress response*. It has served mankind as a protective system by preparing our brains and bodies to urgently handle threats and *perceived* hazards in our environment. Without it, we likely would not have survived as a species. It was triggered in our forefathers when the woolly predators jumped out in front of them, and it's triggered in us today when the driver in the car in front of us slams on his brakes or we hear unexpected footsteps behind us.

Let's take a closer look at how our body's stress response functions. First you become aware of a threat in your environment via one or more of your sensory organs (eyes, ears, touch, taste). Then your central nervous system is alerted and triggers a series of hormonal reactions throughout your body: the adrenals release adrenaline, the hypothalamus releases corticotropin-releasing factor (CRF), the pituitary releases corticotropin, the adrenal cortex releases glucocorticoids and cortisol. Your body responds to this flood of hormones by diverting energy, in the form of blood and glucose, from your digestive system and immune system to your large muscle groups. Your heart rate increases, your muscles tighten, your blood pressure increases, and you breathe faster. This amazing sequence of events is all for the purpose of preparing your body for one of the three Fs—freeze, fight, or flight.

Note: The body's stress response system reacts in the same way to a *perceived* threat as it does to a *real* threat. In other words, it's whether you believe that you do or you don't have control of the circumstances that will determine if it is or is not a stressful event, and your body will react accordingly. This is important to understand; it means that stress is actually in the eye of the beholder.

So, there's good news and there's bad news. The good news is that this remarkable stress response system has carried on throughout our evolution; the bad news is that it was, and still is, meant to be activated *only* on a short-term basis. This is bad news because, in our overworked, over-scheduled lives, we tend to have our stress button in the "on" position more often than not. And your brain and body respond in the *very same way* to the stresses of life-threatening ordeals (physical events) as they do to everyday life pressures (psychological events). Be aware that these seemingly innocent, everyday anxieties (that misunderstanding with your girlfriend, the unpaid bills, the news of future layoffs) all trigger the **same** stress response as a fearsome, shadowy figure chasing you down a dark, lonely alley.

Stress buttons left on raise levels of cortisol, which cause long-term stress, which can have severe health consequences. Physiologically, the increased levels of cortisol eventually lead to injury and destruction of nerve cells, compromised effectiveness of the blood-brain barrier (allowing toxins to enter the brain), an increase in free radicals, and a reduction in the size of the hippocampus (memory formation). The medical community has known for years that long-term or chronic stress can result in devastating health problems: increased blood pressure, sleep problems, depression, obesity, heart disease, digestive disorders, eczema, and memory loss coupled with inability to create new memories.

The results of a recent study at the University of California, Irvine, provided the first evidence that even short-term stress may have the same harmful effects as long-term stress, including impaired cellular communication in the hippocampus (seat of learning and memory). The importance of managing our stress levels is becoming more and more apparent.

Life Stressors. We experience both external and internal stressors. Examples of externally caused stressors are family issues, financial concerns, work-related problems, relationship problems, noise levels, and other major life changes (see Table 8.1). Internal life stressors include attitude, unrealistic expectations of others, and unrealistic expectations of ourselves. Our internal stresses are self-engendered—centered on our own perceptions, which, of course, are based on our past experiences and

TABLE 8.1 Top 10 External Life Stressors
Death of a spouse
Divorce
Marital separation
Jail term
Death of a close family member
Personal injury or illness
Marriage
Job termination
Marital reconciliation
Retirement

Adapted from "Holmes-Rahe Life Changes Scale," by T. H. Homes and R. H. Rahe, *Journal of Psychosomatic Research*, Vol. 11 (1967): 213–18.

subsequent beliefs held concerning those experiences. What causes one person stress can actually be enjoyable to another. For instance, in one of the authors' offices, most clients enjoy the tranquil sounds of the trickling water coming from the wall-mounted water fountain. And yet for one client, a former property manager, the fountain has to be unplugged. The sound stresses her out because it reminds her of broken water pipes and the resulting water damage.

Stress Busters: How to Balance and Harmonize the Body and Brain. Managing stress is about how you *respond*, not react, to your life events. Reactions are intrinsic, but your intellect allows you to choose how you respond. First and foremost, it's essential to take command of your thoughts. Become acutely aware of the thoughts running through your mind and try to establish a sense of control over what thoughts you *allow* to flow through your mind. If there's anything you can control in this life, it's that.

Recognize what opportunities you have to take charge of your attitude, your emotions, your schedule, and your environment. Some stressful situations you may have the power to change. And when you encounter those unwanted unchangeable situations, you can use the power of your thoughts to change your reaction to the situation.

Also, take the time to take care of yourself. Following are some of the time-tested methods of nurturing your brain, body, and spirit:

- **Yoga:** Originating in India, it is a practice of movement, poses, and stretches performed to achieve a balance and union of the mind, body, and spirit.
- **Tai chi:** A form of Chinese martial arts using slow, smooth movements.
- **Qigong:** Pronounced "chee-gung," it means "vital force energy." Originating in China, it consists of exercises, poses, breathing techniques, and meditation.
- **Meditation:** Performing a mental dicipline, such as focusing on a single point of reference, to obtain a deeply relaxed and peaceful state of mind.

- **Progressive muscle relaxation:** An anxiety-reducing technique that consists of progressively isolating individual muscle groups, voluntarily tensing them for 8 to 10 seconds, and then relaxing them.
- **Hypnotherapy:** An artificially induced altered state of consciousness, characterized by heightened suggestibility and receptivity to direction.
- **Neurofeedback:** Also referred to as *neurotherapy, neurobiofeedback,* or *EEG biofeedback,* this is a therapeutic technique that presents the user with real-time feedback on brain wave activity, as measured by electrode sensors on the scalp. Often used to treat ADHD, but also used for stress, PTSD, depression, and addictions.
- **Music:** Music has been shown to have numerous therapeutic benefits, from relieving stress and pain to regulating breathing, lowering both cholesterol and blood pressure, and increasing the body's immune defenses. It has been used by therapists and medical professionals to decrease the effects of chronic pain, depression, grief, and anger. Music therapist Mark Arnold states, "Of course music is beneficial—just sing a lullaby to a child and watch the wonderful effects."
- **Laughter:** The antistress healing effects of laughter are well recognized; it's even been known to relieve chronic pain. Norman Cousins, the man who laughed his way to wellness, wrote of his healing journey through laugh therapy in his book *Anatomy of an Illness as Perceived by the Patient.*
- **Socializing (especially with positive people):** Human interaction is a significant factor in reducing stress and increasing health and longevity.
- **Getting back to nature:** Exposure to nature has proved so helpful in stress reduction that plants and other elements of nature are now commonplace in many hospitals and centers. Nature has also been shown to enhance the immune system.

The Gift of Nourishment

Can what we eat affect our brains and their performance? Indeed it can. Not only does a healthy eating regime support and fortify our heart, lungs, kidneys, and immune system, it also strengthens our nervous system, including our brain. Not surprisingly, the stomach, which is often referred to as the *second brain*, influences the health and performance of our first brain.

Following are just a few foods packed full of the essential vitamins and minerals considered to be nourishing for the mind and body:

- **Cocoa and dark chocolate:** filled with flavonoids that fight the destructive effects of free radicals, which cause cellular oxidative damage in the body and brain.
- **Citrus fruits:** filled with flavonoids, which fight free radicals.
- **Açaí (an exotic fruit):** full of antioxidants—great brain food.
- **Green tea:** another great antioxidant that protects the brain.
- **Blueberries:** shown to improve short-term memory.
- **Turmeric:** the major ingredient in curry, it possesses powerful anti-inflammatory properties and helps clear amyloid beta (the plaque related to Alzheimer's disease).
- **Cranberries:** help preserve brain cells.
- **Fish:** high in omega-3s, a necessity for healthy brain function. Omega-3s reduce inflammation and improve memory.
- **Tomatoes:** contain the antioxidant lycopene, especially useful for protecting the heart and brain.
- **Whole grains (wheat bran, wheat germ):** contain vitamin E, which helps with memory and concentration.
- **Green leafy vegetables (especially spinach and kale):** filled with folic acid, which helps improve memory.
- **Pumpkin seeds:** contain zinc—good for memory.
- **Water:** drink eight glasses of pure water a day (remember, your brain consists of 78 percent water); be wary of storing water for long periods of time or freezing water in plastic containers—polychlorinated biphenyls (PCBs) can leach into the water.

In a study conducted by University of Nottingham professor Ian Macdonald, as reported by *ScienceDaily* (2/07), it was found that "eating chocolate could help to sharpen the mind and give a short-term boost to cognitive skills." A chocolate lover's dream come true!

Brain Aerobics

Neuroplasticity—what an amazing gift! Our brains possess the ability to change physically based on external stimuli—to improve or to worsen. This incredible feature enables our brains to establish new neuro-net pathways or neural networks and offers us the amazing opportunity to rewire and therefore improve our brain fitness throughout our entire life (yes, even over-60 brains.) What's it take? It seems that there are some basic criteria to *optimally* promote neuroplasticity.

Some of them include new and challenging experiences that are fun and rewarding and incorporate multiple senses (vision, sound, taste, touch). Intensive and repetitive behavior also reinforce neuroplasticity. Many of the brain-training software programs attempt to incorporate as many of these criteria as possible. But there are also numerous simpler activities you can easily integrate into your lifestyle. Suggestions: learn a new musical instrument (or your first one); learn a new language; learn new dance steps; travel; join a club; take a class at your local college/YMCA/center, attend lectures; visit museums; do crossword puzzles and Sudoku; or pick up another new hobby. All these activities build new neuro-net connections in your brain, keeping it active, growing, and strong.

Alternatively, you can go straight to the software! If you're attracted to computer games, you're in luck, because many brain-training games are available. SharpBrains.com (which, by the way, is one of most outstanding sites for accurate, up-to-date, and entertaining information on the brain) estimates that the U.S. brain-training software industry increased from $100 million in 2005 to $225 million in 2007. Here are a few of the more popular brain-training websites: lumosity.com, neurogizers.com, emwave .com, happy-neuron.com, and mybraintrainer.com.

These software programs vary as much in their designs as they do in their claims to enhance the learners' performance. The verdict is still out on the extent of the beneficial effects of some of the games and the integrity

of the manufacturers' claims to these benefits. You will want to check the most recent research before making your investment.

To help keep a sharp, clear, crisp, flexible, and strong brain, stay open to new ideas, approaches, resources, and learning. Remain active both physically and socially—your brain will love you for it. Don't allow the stresses of life to control your thoughts; try to relax and limit worry as much as you can. Most important, maintain a positive outlook. If you're the owner of a positive attitude, you possess a powerful tool that will help ensure that the changes in your brain's neuroplasticity (the brain's ability to reorganize itself based on environmental input) will be positive, strong, and long-lasting.

Mind Mapping

Materials

Mind Mapping Sample handout (provided)

Time

15 to 20 minutes

Procedure

Initially developed by brainpower expert Tony Buzan, this free-flowing method of capturing ideas is a great way to harness the brain's power of associative thinking. It allows anyone to graphically chart the essence of a talk or presentation.

Explain how mind mapping works: essentially, you're creating an idea map wherein the central idea of the talk is drawn or written in the center of the paper and then, as the presentation continues, you continue to add branches representing relevant ideas that come to mind.

·Display the Mind Mapping Sample. Suggest to the participants that they try this exercise individually for the next few minutes, mapping the topic you are presenting. Continue with your presentation and then solicit feedback from the group at the end.

Discussion Questions

1. Did you find this to be an easy way to take notes?

2. What were some of the creative ways you did so?

3. Have you used this or a similar technique in the past?

Mind Mapping Sample

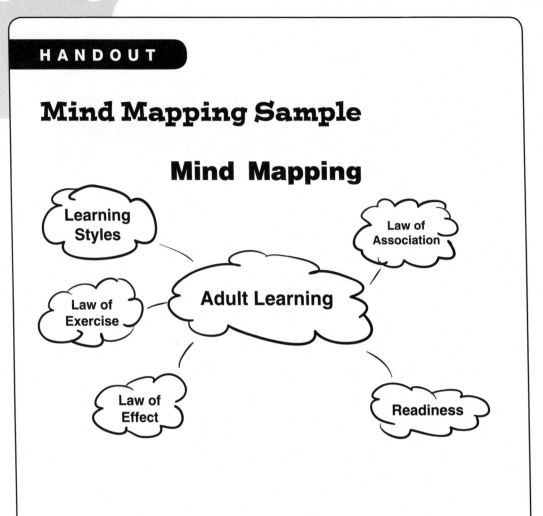

Mind Mapping

Learning Styles

Law of Association

Law of Exercise

Adult Learning

Law of Effect

Readiness

Want to Be a Genius?

OBJECTIVES
- To give participants a chance to "show their stuff"
- To exercise the brain by giving it a good challenge

Materials

Copies of the IQ Quiz handout (provided)

Time

10 to 15 minutes

Procedure

That most of us really never stop learning is a given in today's society. Distribute copies of the IQ Quiz and ask participants to work in groups of two as they go through the questions. Let them know that these are not easy questions, but they may surprise themselves with how easily the answers come. Allow a few minutes and then ask for their answers.

Discussion Questions

1. Were some of you surprised at how easy you found some of these questions?

2. Did any of you just give up? Have you ever experienced a challenge that seemed impossible and then, after you gave your brain a break, the answer just came to you?

3. Did you find that working with a partner brought a different perspective to things?

IQ Quiz

Here's a challenge for you. Put on your thinking caps and get your brain in high gear as you go through these questions.

1. How many buttons are on a touch-tone phone? _____

2. How many of those numbers have four letters? _____

3. Which ones? _____

4. How many—and which—symbols show no numbers?
   _____

5. Which letters are missing in this sequence? _____ S _____ T _____
   T _____

6. On which playing card is the card maker's trademark? _____

7. What do these words have in common? _____

   Dresser   Potato   Uneven
   Banana   Revive   Grammar

8. Make four 9s equal 100. _____

9. Make six 9s equal 100. _____

10. Jackie is twice as old as Robert. In five years, Robert will be the
    same age as Jackie is now. How old are they now? Jackie is _____;
    Robert is _____.

11. What's the next number in this sequence? 2 2 4 12 48 _____

12. How many states in the United States start with the letter A? _____

13. Which word in English is most often misspelled? _____

14. Six boys can eat 12 hot dogs in one hour. At that rate, how many hot dogs can four boys down in two hours? _____

15. The world population is roughly _____ billion.

16. In a leap year, how many months have 29 days in them? _____

17. What are the top five countries in population? _____
_____ _____ _____ _____

18. Which five countries are the largest in size? _____
_____ _____ _____ _____

19. Which country has the most births annually? _____

20. What commonly used English word changes its pronunciation when capitalized? _____

IQ Quiz Answers

1. How many buttons are on a touch-tone phone? **12**

2. How many of those numbers have four letters? **2**

3. Which ones? **7 and 9**

4. How many—and which—symbols show no numbers? **2—star and pound keys**

5. Which letters are missing in this sequence? **S** S **M** T **W** T **F** (days of week starting with Saturday)

6. On which playing card is the card maker's trademark? **Ace of spades**

7. What do these words have in common? **Take the first letter of each word and place it at the end and the word spells the same backward.**

   Dresser   Potato   Uneven
   Banana   Revive   Grammar

8. Make four 9s equal 100. **99 9/9= 100**

9. Make six 9s equal 100. **99 99/99 =100**

10. Jackie is twice as old as Robert. In five years, Robert will be the same age as Jackie is now. How old are they now? Jackie is **10**; Robert is **5**

11. What's the next number in this sequence? 2 2 4 12 48 **240** (each number is multiplied by 1 and then 2, 3, 4, 5)

12. How many states in the Unites States start with the letter A? **Four: Alaska, Alabama, Arizona, Arkansas**

13. Which word in English is most often misspelled? **Misspelled**

14. Six boys can eat 12 hot dogs in one hour. At that rate, how many hot dogs can four boys down in two hours? **16**

15. The world population is roughly **6.8** billion.

16. In a leap year, how many months have 29 days in them? **12**

17. What are the top five countries in population? **China, India, United States, Indonesia, and Brazil**

18. Which five countries are the largest in size? **Russia, Canada, China, United States, and Brazil**

19. Which country has the most births annually? **India**

20. What commonly used English word changes its pronunciation when capitalized? **polish/Polish**

Stress-Stress-Stress!

OBJECTIVES
- To appreciate the personal impact of changes caused by industry adjustments, economic changes, and environmental modifications
- To appreciate how these changes can translate into stress
- To discuss possible stress relief techniques

Materials

Flip charts, markers, pens, paper, Post-It notes in four different colors (enough for 10 of each color for each participant), colored stars

Time

25 to 30 minutes

Procedure

We are seeing big changes in almost every industry, often translating to changes in one's own job respon-sibilities. It's a situation ripe for tension and stress! This activity explores four separate areas: changes, emotions, results, and solutions.

1. **Changes:** Identify and list all the changes that are taking place in your partici-pants' industries (increased competition, fewer resources, longer work hours). Capture items on the flip chart under the title "Changes in Our Industries." After all changes are listed, ask participants to identify all the "change" items listed on the flip chart that *personally* affect them. Ask them to write all of those "change" items on green Post-It notes and to then affix those notes to their clothing (they can go anywhere—scattered all over the upper torso or up and down the legs).

2. **Emotions:** Ask participants to identify all the emotions that the items listed on the "Changes in Our Industries" are causing them (anger, fear, frustration, etc.). Capture the list of emotions on the flip chart under the title "Emotions Caused by the Changes." After all emotions are listed, ask participants to identify all the "emotional" items listed on the flip chart that they *personally*

relate to. Ask then to write all of those items on blue Post-It notes and to then affix those notes to their clothing.

3. **Results or Consequences:** Identify all the results or consequences that arise from the impact of the industry changes and the emotional consequences related to those changes (increased stress, health issues, longer working hours, relationship strain, less time with children, loss of $$$$) and record these items on the flip chart under the title "Consequences." After all "consequences" are listed, ask participants to identify all the "consequence" items listed on the flip chart that *personally* relate to them. Ask them to write each of these items on yellow Post-It notes and to then affix those notes to their clothing.

Before moving on to step 4, ask participants (who likely are now covered in assorted colored Post-It notes) to roam about the room comparing "notes" with other participants. Allow approximately three minutes (more time with larger groups).

4. **Don't Worry—Be Happy:** Have participants identify all the methods or techniques they have found or heard of that assist in relieving or reducing these stresses (meditation, exercise, happy movie, walks with family members, deep breathing) and record these items on the flip chart under the title "Solutions" (or "Don't Worry—Be Happy.") After all "solutions" are listed, ask participants to identify all the "solutions" items listed on the flip chart that they *personally* use or are considering using. Ask them to write each of these items on pink Post-It notes and then to affix colored stars to the notes (because they should be congratulated for taking care of themselves, which has to happen before they can properly care for others). Then have them affix those Post-It notes—with stars—to their clothing.

Discussion Questions

1. Were you surprised to realize how much you are coping with?
2. Were you surprised to see how many others have the same stresses as you?
3. What were your biggest *ah-has* from this experience?
4. What are your favorite/most effective techniques for dealing with stress? (Meditation, deep breathing, yoga, and exercise are just a few examples. What else?)

The Psychology of Change

OBJECTIVE
- To explore some of the states of mind we experience when undergoing a serious change or challenge

Materials
None
Time
10 to 15 minutes

Procedure

Explain to your participants that Elisabeth Kübler-Ross's grief research suggests that we go through some definitive steps or stages when facing serious change. When changes translate into loss, we tend to grieve that which we no longer have (be it a job or a loved one).

The Stages of Loss

1. Denial
2. Anger
3. Bargaining
4. Depression
5. Acceptance

Show these stages on a flip chart or PowerPoint slide. Explain that we all work through these stages during a major loss in our life and that these phases are not necessarily experienced in the order presented here. Some people will experience one or more of the stages several times, switching back and forth among them. We all process change and grief in our own individual manner. There is no one right way or wrong way to grieve, and each person should take as much time as required to grieve in his or her own way. Our ultimate goal, however, is to reach the stage of acceptance.

Form groups of three or four participants and ask them to discuss candidly a time recently when they or someone close to them (family member or coworker) underwent a serious challenge and whether they recognized behaviors or actions they would associate with any of the five stages of loss. Allow 5 to 10 minutes for discussion.

Discussion Questions

1. Would anyone care to share a personal experience?
2. Do you think while you or others are going through a particular stage that you're actually aware of being at that stage?
3. Although we talked about these experiences in a matter of minutes, in real life it could take weeks or even months to work through grief and arrive at the last stage of acceptance. Any examples?

Take a Card, Any Card

OBJECTIVE

- To show that a "group think" activity can actually increase an individual's creative thinking abilities

Materials

One or two decks of playing cards (enough for one card per person)

Time

15 to 20 minutes

Procedure

Pass out one playing card to every person. Form teams of three or four participants and then have them show their card to the others on their team. Their task is to compose a story or lesson on the topic of your program by incorporating all three (or four) cards.

For example, one group has picked the jack of spades, the two of diamonds, and the queen of hearts.

In a customer service class, their story might go something like this: A customer named Jack Spades came into a jewelry store and wanted to buy two small diamonds for his fiancée. He wanted to have these made into earrings for his bride-to-be, whom he affectionately referred to as the queen of his heart.

Give them five minutes to work on this and then ask each group to present its story. The story can take the form of a cheer, a poem, a lesson, etc., as their own creativity provides.

Discussion Questions

1. How easy was it once you got things going?

2. Did you find it fun as you started building your story and trying to make some sense out of it?

3. Can you see how the brain quickly picks up on others' thoughts and can easily assimilate these into new patterns?

4. Are there ways you can use these group-think techniques in solving some challenges at work?

Communication Styles

OBJECTIVE
- To learn how to deal with different types of personalities

Materials

Copies of the Working with Communication Styles
handout (provided)

Time

20 to 25 minutes

Procedure

Ask how many in the group have previously taken a personality assessment such as the Myers-Briggs. Assuming that many, if not most, have, inform them that they will shortly be using a similar tool. Explain that this exercise will help them understand more about their personality style and preferences, as well as the styles and preferences of others who may differ from them. Suggest that sometimes, when we encounter individuals we think of as being "difficult," they are simply individuals whose turn-ons and turnoffs differ from ours.

Distribute copies of the Working with Communication Styles handout and ask participants to review the four communication styles (amiable, analytical, driver, and expressive). Based on the few traits listed under each style, ask participants to make a quick judgment as to which of these styles they're most likely to identify with. After participants have identified their communication style, ask that they gather in their "style" groups.

Tip

Depending on the size of the group, we recommend no more than five to six people in each "style" group; if necessary, further subdivide the group. Each of the four groups will now focus on identifying the typical turn-ons and turnoffs of their particular communication style.

Discussion Questions

1. When you discussed the items with your fellow personality styles, was it fairly easy to get consensus?
2. Were you thinking of specific people at work that fit these categories? Were your discussions helpful?
3. Which of these styles describes your manager? Are you now more aware of ways to work with his or her style?
4. How can you work better with other styles at work?

Working with Communication Styles

These four social styles identify different patterns of behavior. Discuss with your peers those traits, characteristics, values, etc., you share with one another. Then for each trait listed for your group's personality/communication style, identify a turn-on and a turnoff regarding the way others treat you or interact with you.

Amiable

Typical Traits	*Turn-Ons*	*Turnoffs*
Friendly	_____	_____
Congenial	_____	_____
Cooperative	_____	_____

Analytical

Typical Traits	*Turn-Ons*	*Turnoffs*
Methodical	_____	_____
Soft-Spoken	_____	_____
Neat, Organized	_____	_____

Driver

Typical Traits	*Turn-Ons*	*Turnoffs*
All Business	_____	_____
Moves Fast	_____	_____
Speaks Loudly	_____	_____

Expressive

Typical Traits	Turn-Ons	Turnoffs
People Oriented	_____	_____
Uses Hunches	_____	_____
Animated	_____	_____

Working with Communication Styles Sample Answers

These four social styles identify different patterns of behavior. Discuss with your peers those traits, characteristics, values, etc., you share with one another. Then for each trait listed for your group's personality/communication style, identify a turn-on and a turnoff regarding the way others treat you or interact with you.

Amiable

Typical Traits	Turn-Ons	Turnoffs
Friendly	Including Others	Impersonal
Congenial	Relationships	Non–Team Players
Cooperative	Interpersonal Feelings	Pushy Mannerisms

Analytical

Typical Traits	Turn-Ons	Turnoffs
Methodical	Thoroughness	Careless Individuals
Soft-Spoken	Facts/Figures	Loud/Boisterous
Neat, Organized	Details	Fast Talkers

Driver

Typical Traits	Turn-Ons	Turnoffs
All Business	Always Busy	Slow Talkers
Moves Fast	Bottom Line	Idle Chitchat
Speaks Loudly	Challenges	Ramblers

Expressive

Typical Traits	*Turn-Ons*	*Turnoffs*
People Oriented	Big Picture	Routine
Uses Hunches	Personality	Soft-Spoken
Animated	Excitement	No Eye Contact

Top of the Morning

Materials

None

Time

10 to 15 minutes

Procedure

Explain that the first few minutes or hours of any day often set the tone for the rest of the day. Rushing around in the morning, looking for those car keys, or having difficulty finding the work we brought home last night can set us up for a stressful day. On the other hand, getting things ready the night before and having everything laid out—choice of clothes, bus pass, etc.—can help us start out far more serene and even save us a few minutes in the process. Ask the group to form teams of three or four and discuss these questions:

1. Can you relate to "Where'd I put those darn keys?" syndrome, or are you one of the "always organized, always ready" individuals?
2. Have you noticed that when your day begins with chaos, you tend to have less patience with others—i.e., you're running late, so you become irritated with that driver in front of you who seems to be going soooo slow?

Discussion Questions

1. What are some strategies or methods you've learned to avoid those rushed mornings that you can share with others?
2. Can you share some of those "crazy mornings" you have experienced?
3. What have you learned about yourself from those harried times?

Bibliography

Amen, D. *Change Your Brain, Change Your Life.* New York: Three Rivers Press, 1998.

"Attention." *Mosby's Dental Dictionary,* 2nd ed. (2008). http://medical-dictionary .thefreedictionary.com/attention.

Bartels, L. "10 Brain Tips to Teach and Learn." SharpBrains. http://www.sharp brains.com/blog/2008/07/03/10-brain-training-tips-to-teach-and-learn (accessed February 8, 2009).

Begley, S. *Train Your Mind, Change Your Brain.* New York: Ballantine Books, 2008.

Bland, J. "About Gender: Differences." http://www.gender.org.uk/about/00_diffs .html (accessed February 19, 2009).

Braun, S. *Buzz: The Science and Lore of Alcohol and Caffeine.* New York: Penguin Books, 1997, 40–43.

Brizendine, L. *The Female Brain.* New York: Broadway Books, 2006.

Campbell, D. "D'oh! Brain Scientists Unravel Mystery of Absent-Mindedness." *Guardian* (July 2007). http://www.guardian.co.uk/science/2007/jul/29/1/ print (accessed February 20, 2009).

"Cerebrum." Wikipedia. http://en.wikipedia.org/wiki/Tenecephalon (accessed February 22, 2009).

Clark, D. "Left Brain Right Brain—a Myth" (June 18, 2007). http://donaldclark planb.blogspot.com/2007/06/left-brain-right-brain-myth.html (accessed February 7, 2009).

Demos, J. *Getting Started with Neurofeedback*, New York: W. W. Norton & Company, 2005.

Derichs-Kunstmann, K. "Women Learn Differently." http://www.uni-ulm.de/ LiLL/5.0/E/5.3/women.html (accessed February 2009).

Doidge, N. *The Brain that Changes Itself.* New York: Penguin Books, 2007.

Dufty, D. "Ten Myths About the Brain." http://www.time-etc.com/2007/06/ ten-myths-about-brain.html (accessed February 2, 2009).

Erickson, K., et al. "Aerobic Fitness Is Associated with Hippocampal Volume in Elderly Humans." *Hippocampus.* Doi:10.1002/hipo.20547 (2009). http://www.ncbi.nlm.nih.gov/pubmed/19123237.

Fehmi, L., and J. Robbins. *The Open Focus Brain.* Boston: Trumpeter, 2007.

Freer, P. "Current Brain Research." Play Attention (2004): http://www.playattention.com/brain-research (accessed January 22, 2009).

"Girls Learn Differently." http://www.girlslearndifferently.com/learningstyles.html. (accessed February 2, 2009).

Grant, R. "Brain Foods." *The Cornell Daily Sun*, February 23, 2009. http://cornellsun.com/print/35445 (accessed February 24, 2009).

Hanson, D. "Does Drinking Alcohol Kill Brain Cells?" Potsdam University (2007). http://www2.potsdam.edu/hansondj/HealthIssues/110362109.html (accessed February 7, 2009).

Hitti, M. "Men, Women Use Brain Differently: One Way Isn't Necessarily Better Than the Other, Small Study Shows." Medscape (December 2005). http://www.medscape.com/viewarticle/518346 (accessed February 15, 2009).

Holladay, A. "Does Alcohol Kill Brain Cells?" Wonderquest (2008). http://www.wonderquest.com/BrainCells.html (accessed February 22, 2009).

"How Do We Learn and Remember?" Brain Science (November 2003). http://www.brainscience.brown.edu/research/6questions/how_do_we_learn.html (accessed February 8, 2009).

Howard, P. J. *The Owner's Manual for the Brain: Everyday Applications from Mind-Brain Research.* 3rd ed. Austin: Bard Press, 2006.

"Human Memory." NASA. http://human-factors.arc.nasa.gov/cognition/tutorials/ModelOf/Knowmore1.html (accessed February 7, 2009).

"Human Memory." College of Computing at Georgia Tech. http://www.cc.gatech.edu/classes/cs6751_97_winter/Topics/human-cap/memory.html (accessed February 7, 2009).

Jaffe-Gill, E., et al. "Improving your Memory." Help Guide (2007). http://www.helpguide.org/life/improving_memory.html (accessed February 12, 2009).

Jensen, E. *Brain-Based Learning: The New Paradigm of Teaching.* 2nd ed. Thousand Oaks, CA: Corwin Press, 2008.

Jensen, G. B., and B. Pakkenberg. "Do Alcoholics Drink their Neurons Away?" *The Lancet,* 342(8881)(1993), 1201–1204.

Kishore, L. "Do Men and Women Learn Differently?" Meri News (August 28, 2008). http://www.merinews.com/catFull.jsp?articleID=14198 (accessed February 15, 2009).

Klemm, B. "Getting from Here to There: Making Memory Consolidation Work." SharpBrains (July 7, 2008). http://www.sharpbrains.com/tag/memory-consolidation (accessed February 2, 2009).

Kolpack, D. "Microsoft Explores Educational Link to Video Games." *USA Today*, February 20, 2009.

"Lateralization of Brain Function." Wikipedia. http://en.wikipedia.org/wiki/Lateralization_of_brain_function (accessed February 22, 2009).

Latham, C. "Brain Coach Answers: How Can I Improve My Memory? Is There a Daily Exercise I Can Do to Improve It?" SharpBrains (November 6, 2006) http://www.sharpbrains.com/blog/2006/11/06/ (accessed February 7, 2009).

"Learning, Memory, and Language" Society for Neuroscience (2008). http://www.sfn.org/skins/main/pdf/brainfacts/2008/learning-memory-language.pdf (accessed February 12, 2009).

"The Left Brain/ Right Brain" Myth. Science Blogs (October 13, 2007). http://www.scienceblogs.com/neurophilosophy/2007/10/the_left_brain_right_brain_myt.php (accessed February 4, 2009).

Legato, M. "Why Men Never Remember and Women Never Forget: The Secrets to Better Communication." *Bottom Line/Personal* (September 1, 2006), 13–14.

Matlin, M. W. "Bimbos and Rambos: The Cognitive Basis of Gender Stereotypes" (1998). http://www.psichi.org/pubs/articles/article_112.aspx (accessed July 6, 2009).

McPherson, F. "The Role of Emotion in Memory." Memory Key (2004). http://memory-key.com/NatureofMemory/emotion.htm (accessed February 25, 2009).

McPherson, F. "Action Slips." Memory Key (2006). http://www.memory-key.com/EverydayMemory/slips.html (accessed February 12, 2009.)

McPherson, F. "Multitasking." Memory Key (2006). http://www.memory-key.com/EverydayMemory/multitasking.html (accessed February 12, 2009).

McPherson, F. "Tip-of-the-Tongue Experiences." Memory Key (2006). http://www.memory-key.com/EverydayMemory/TOT.html. (accessed February 12, 2009).

Medina, J. *Brain Rules*. Seattle: Pear Press, 2008.

"Memory." Wikipedia. http://en.wikipedia.org/wiki/Memory (accessed February 15, 2009).

"Myths About Aging and the Brain." AARP. http://www.aarp.org/health/brain/aging/myths_about_aging_and_the_brain.html (accessed February 4, 2009).

National Institute for Physiological Sciences. "How Is Our Left Brain Different From Our Right?" *ScienceDaily* (November 25, 2008). http://www.sciencedaily.com/releases/2008/11/081117192918.html (accessed March 9, 2009).

Patterson, J. "Female Perception vs. Male Perception." Lifescript (May 1, 2007). http://www.lifescript.com/Life/Relationships/Marriage/Female_Perception_vs_Male_Perception.aspx (accessed March 11, 2009).

Pease, B., and A. Pease. *Why Men Don't Listen and Women Can't Read Maps: How We Are Different and What to Do About It.* New York: Broadway Books, 1998.

"Please! May I Have Your Attention?" Memory Key (December 2008). http://www.memory-key.com/neurology/Attention_news.htm (accessed February 12, 2009).

Ratey, J. J. *A User's Guide to the Brain.* New York: Vintage Books, 2002.

Ratey, J. J., and E. Hagerman. *Spark—The Revolutionary New Science of Exercise and the Brain.* New York: Little Brown and Company, 2008.

"Researchers Identify New Form of Superior Memory Syndrome." *ScienceDaily* (March 14, 2006). http://sciencedaily.com/releases/2006/03/060314085102.htm (accessed February 7, 2009).

Restak, R. *The Naked Brain.* New York: Three Rivers Press, 2006.

Restak, R. *The New Brain.* New York: Rodale, 2003.

Sax, L. "Why Gender Matters" (2005). http://www.whygendermatters.com (accessed February 14, 2009).

Schardt, D. "Exercising the Mind: Psychologist K. Warner Schaie: Interview" (May 1997). http://findarticles.com/p/articles/mi_m0813/is_n4_v24/ai_19396013/ (accessed January 9, 2009).

Sousa, D. A. *How the Brain Learns.* 3rd ed. Thousand Oaks, CA: Corwin Press, 2006.

Sperry, R. "The Split Brain Experiments." http://nobelprize.org/educational_games/medicine/split-brain/background.html (accessed February 4, 2009).

Swingle, P. *Biofeedback for the Brain.* New Jersey: Rutgers University Press, 2008.

Taylor, J. B. *My Stroke of Insight.* New York: Viking Penguin, 2006.

University of Illinois at Urbana-Champaign. "Physical Fitness Improves Spatial Memory, Increases Size of Brain Structure." *ScienceDaily* (March 3, 2009).

Van Wagner, K. "Memory Retrieval: Retrieving Information from Memory." *Cognitive Psychology* (2009). http://psychology.about.com/od/cognitivepsychology/a/memory_retrival.htm?p=1 (accessed February 14, 2009).

Vernon, D., et al. "The Effect of Training Distinct Neurofeedback Protocols on Aspects of Cognitive Performance." *International Journal of Psychophysiology* 47 (2003): 75–85.

"Visual Brain Areas Play Vital Role in Short-term Memory, Says Study" Canadian Broadcasting Centre (February 2009). http://www.cbc.ca/technology/story/2009/02/18/fmri-memory.html (accessed February 19, 2009).

Ward, L. M. "Attention." *Scholarpedia* (2008) 3(10), 1538.

Weil, A. *Healthy Aging: A Lifelong Guide to Your Physical and Spiritual Well-Being.* New York: Alfred A. Knopf, 2005.

Weil, A., and G. Small. *The Healthy Brain Kit Workbook.* Boulder, CO: Sounds True, 2007.

About the Authors

Founder and CEO of the Optimum Brain Institute in Tempe, Arizona, **Carol A. Burnett** brings to her clients and audiences a wide range of experience and expertise. Her passion for the field of neurofeedback and the profound transformations it has produced for her clients has inspired her to advance this noninvasive, promising mode of optimizing one's brain and quality of life. Carol has the unique ability to translate state-of-the-art brain theory and research into practical learning experiences. Adapting the newest and most exciting cutting-edge concepts, she transfers these scholarly research findings in bio-energy fields into understandable and personal applications.

Coupled with a strong academic and corporate background, she has taught and consulted for colleges in the United States and Canada. In addition to having two undergraduate degrees, she also holds a master's degree in educational counseling psychology from the State University of New York. She has served as an assistant vice president for a national financial institution and has worked extensively in the field of human resources.

As a nationally recognized consultant and educator, Carol has conducted seminars and workshops for hundreds of clients. She has earned several nationally recognized certifications including Myers-Briggs, DDI (Development Dimensions, International), and The Institute of Cultural Affairs' Group Facilitation Methods. A member of the Association of Applied Psychophysiology and Biofeedback, she is also a master practitioner of neuro-linguistic programming and has been certified as a registered hypnotherapist in the United States and Canada. Having been Third Degree Reiki certified, she is also a certified Transformational

Workshop Leader for the Louise Hay Methods. Carol can be contacted at Carol@OptimumBrainInstitute.com

An active member of the National Speakers Association, **Edward E. Scannell** has given more than a thousand presentations, seminars, and workshops across the United States and internationally.

He has written or coauthored 20 books and more than 100 articles in the fields of HRD, Creativity, Team Building, and Management. He has served as ASTD's (American Society for Training and Development) National President and also as Executive Chairman for IFTDO (International Federation of Training and Development Organizations).

A past president of MPI's (Meeting Professionals International) Arizona chapter, he was elected as MPI's International President in 1990. He was named MPI's International Planner of the Year in 1995 and was inducted into the Convention Industry Council's Hall of Leaders in 2007.

Ed was elected National President of the National Speakers Association (NSA) in 1991–92 and received NSA's highest honor, the Cavett award, in 1999.

He is currently serving as the Director of the Center for Professional Development and Training in Scottsdale, Arizona. Ed can be reached at EESAZ@aol.com